NEW DIRECTIONS FOR PROGRAM EVALUATION
A Publication of the American Evaluation Association

William R. Shadish, *Memphis State University*
EDITOR-IN-CHIEF

Understanding Causes and Generalizing About Them

Lee B. Sechrest
University of Arizona

Anne G. Scott
University of Arizona

EDITORS

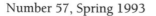

D0829919

Number 57, Spring 1993

JOSSEY-BASS PUBLISHERS
San Francisco

UNDERSTANDING CAUSES AND GENERALIZING ABOUT THEM
Lee B. Sechrest, Anne G. Scott (eds.)
New Directions for Program Evaluation, no. 57
William R. Shadish, Editor-in-Chief

Microfilm copies of issues and articles are available in 16mm and 35mm, as well as microfiche in 105mm, through University Microfilms Inc., 300 North Zeeb Road, Ann Arbor, Michigan 48106.

LC 85-644749   ISSN 0164-7989   ISBN 1-55542-696-4

NEW DIRECTIONS FOR PROGRAM EVALUATION is part of The Jossey-Bass Education Series and is published quarterly by Jossey-Bass Inc., Publishers (publication number USPS 449-050).

EDITORIAL CORRESPONDENCE should be sent to the editor-in-chief, William R. Shadish, Department of Psychology, Memphis State University, Memphis, Tennessee 38152.

INSTRUCTIONS TO CONTRIBUTORS

NEW DIRECTIONS FOR PROGRAM EVALUATION (NDPE), a quarterly sourcebook, is an official publication of the American Evaluation Association. As such, NDPE publishes empirical, methodological, and theoretical work on all aspects of program evaluation and related fields. Substantive areas may include any area of social programming such as mental health, education, job training, medicine, or public health, but may also extend the boundaries of evaluation to such topics as product evaluation, personnel evaluation, policy analysis, or technology assessment. In all cases, the focus on evaluation is more important than the particular substantive topic.

NDPE does not consider or publish unsolicited single manuscripts. Each issue of NDPE is devoted to a single topic, with contributions solicited, organized, reviewed, and edited by a guest editor. Issues may take any of several forms, such as a series of related chapters, a monograph, or a long article followed by brief critical commentaries. In all cases, proposals must follow a specific format, which can be obtained from the editor-in-chief. These proposals are sent to members of the editorial board, and to relevant substantive experts, for peer review. This process may result in rejection, acceptance, or a recommendation to revise and resubmit. However, NDPE is committed to working constructively with potential guest editors to help them develop acceptable proposals. Close contact with the editor-in-chief is encouraged during proposal preparation and generation.

COPIES OF NDPE's "Guide for Proposal Development" and "Proposal Format" can be obtained from the editor-in-chief:

William R. Shadish, Editor-in-Chief
New Directions for Program Evaluation
Department of Psychology
Memphis State University
Memphis, TN 38152
Office: 901-678-4687
FAX: 901-678-2579
Bitnet: SHADISHWR@MEMSTVX1

CONTENTS

EDITORS' NOTES

Program evaluators, particularly those working in the social and behavioral areas, almost always rely on nonexperimental data for their evaluations, not so much as a matter of choice but rather because of practical, ethical, or other considerations. Even when it is possible to use randomized experimental designs, often the end result is not optimal, and other nonexperimental approaches are needed to aid in the interpretation of the results. Because of the reliance on nonexperimental methods in social-behavioral evaluations, the development of sound methods for interpreting the results is crucial. Methods to be improved involve all aspects of the evaluation, beginning with the design and setup of the research and moving on to data collection and analyses and, finally, to the interpretation of results.

At the same time, most of the subject areas investigated by evaluators (for example, social-behavioral research, medical services, and education) are complex. This complexity is partly due to the great variation among subjects, as well as variation in the components of a program and actual implementation of the program. A major problem arises when evaluators and decision makers assume that findings from one study generalize across similar programs in other parts of the country with different sets of populations. The issue of generalization is one that every evaluator needs to take into account, both when conducting their research and when reporting results.

The two chapters presented in this volume, *Understanding Causes and Generalizing About Them*, address the issue of theory in evaluation. The use of theory in program evaluations is usually implicit in the sense that we choose which variables to include in our studies and which to leave out. On the other hand, variables are often included out of habit, because of the availability of existing measures or because the variables make for easy data collection. The biggest problem with selecting variables that are convenient is that we may end up with an artificially constricted view of what is going on in the field in question. One popular example from higher education is when evaluators in their assessment of what best predicts attrition or grade point average in a group of students include such variables as age, ethnicity, sex, and test scores, which are readily available measures, and ignore what might be major factors that are more difficult to define and measure, such as motivation and personal conflicts involving work, family, and nonacademic career opportunities. By continuing to rely on the same measures in study after study, we are limiting our scope of inquiry and ultimately our understanding of a problem.

In Chapter One, Lipsey begins by offering an alternative to the traditional approach of focusing only on outcomes for different treatment groups, without any thought to what goes on within the treatment. Not only does an evaluation focusing on outcomes limit our understanding of a phenomenon, it also may provide misleading information, or information that is limited in the circumstances in which it is relevant. Our methods are often so crude that we miss the subtleties that are necessary to truly understand a phenomenon. Lipsey insists that evaluators conduct theory-driven research, which means that theory is necessary during all aspects of an evaluation. Evaluators must begin by considering whether the treatment is even plausible and go on to examine subject or population issues, the methods used, and, ultimately, the interpretation of the results. The strength of Lipsey's approach is that it offers researchers and policymakers much more information, which is particularly helpful when a specific program does not "work." Theory, in this chapter, refers to "small theory" in that the focus is on the explanation of processes specific to the program being evaluated, as opposed to an overall larger theory encompassing the entire field being studied. This distinction makes Lipsey's approach less intimidating and more doable.

In Chapter Two, Cook continues this discussion, beginning with some of the Cronbach's (1982) stipulations of meeting the criteria for causal interpretation. Sampling theory is demonstrated to be rarely practical when causal connections are to be generalized. Cook brings up many of the problems associated with meeting these criteria in real-life situations, such as the problems encountered by program evaluators. An alternative strategy is suggested by Cook to address these issues adequately, specifically, the summarizing of results across multiple studies through such methods as meta-analysis. The advantage of this approach is that although a single study cannot satisfy all of Cronbach's tenets, it is possible to satisfy them by looking across studies. This synthetic approach also allows the researcher to explore the variability in effect sizes found in different studies and to determine, perhaps, what accounts for large or small effects. Of course, all methods have limitations, and Cook discusses these as well. Some limitations, however, can be traced back to the lack of a theory-driven approach. For example, without a theoretical understanding of a treatment, it is not possible to determine whether studies being combined contain the same bias.

Together, the two chapters in this volume address the importance of producing results that are both interpretable and generalizable, and therefore that increase knowledge in a given area of research. In short, evaluators need to be heavily involved in the programs that they are evaluating, which is too often not the case. In order to more fully understand what the outcomes are, including those not necessarily prespecified, and how to interpret the results, researchers must first acquire a good understanding of the rationale for a program and the characteristics of a sample (both people and settings). Sometimes, a program may change over time, and evaluators cannot be rigid in their evaluation strategy and must change the outcomes being measured accordingly. Evaluations may become more complex, requiring more expertise from the evaluator, but the results will provide more comprehensive and richer interpretations, which in turn lead to a better explanation of how and why a program worked (or did not) as opposed to an all-or-nothing conclusion. Particularly when funds are tight and fewer evaluations are likely to be funded, the knowledge derived from evaluations is more important than ever.

Lee B. Sechrest
Anne G. Scott
Editors

Reference

Cronbach, L. J. *Designing Evaluations of Educational and Social Programs.* San Francisco: Jossey-Bass, 1982.

LEE B. SECHREST *is professor of psychology at the University of Arizona, Tucson.*

ANNE G. SCOTT *received her doctorate in psychology at the University of Arizona and is acting director of the university's Center for Research of Undergraduate Education.*

An overview of the critical issues in theory-driven applied research is presented.

Theory as Method: Small Theories of Treatments

Mark W. Lipsey

This chapter examines the role of theory in strengthening causal interpretation in nonexperimental research. It is, therefore, appropriate to begin with a review of some of the fundamentals of causal inference. Following the models of Holland (1986) and Rubin (1974), a population of units can be assumed, in this case persons, each of whom has potential to be exposed to some event, A, and make some response, B. The central question is whether A causes B. Note that this causal question has meaning only when variation can be observed in event A and the response B, and the nature of any correlation can be examined. If A is a constant condition and B is a constant response, there is only tautology in the claim that A causes B—for example, that gravity causes a person to remain on the earth's surface. When circumstances in which A differs can be compared and it is found that B also differs, it is proper to ask if the relationship is causal.

To answer the causal question, researchers capitalize on the inherent comparative nature of the concept of causality. The circumstance when A is present is compared with the circumstance when it is absent in order to observe whether B regularly occurs in the one case and not in the other. This leads to what Holland (1986) and others call the fundamental prob-

A version of this paper was published in L. Sechrest, E. Perrin, and J. Bunker (eds.), *Research Methodology: Strengthening Causal Interpretations of Nonexperimental Data* (Conference proceedings), Washington, D.C.: Agency for Health Care Policy and Research, Public Health Service, U.S. Department of Health and Human Services, May 1990.

lem of causal inference. In short, it is physically impossible to compare A-present versus A-absent in otherwise identical circumstances.

The closest alternative is to observe A-present versus A-absent at the same time but on different persons and mount a side argument—in particular, a statistical argument—that there are no important differences among persons. Another option is to observe A-present versus A-absent on the same persons but at different times and argue stability—that is, that there are no important differences among the circumstances occurring at those different times. This point is fundamental. It is what makes causality an inference rather than a fact.

If time could be rolled back and events manipulated as required, causal relations could be established as a matter of observation with the same factual status as any other observation (Reichardt, 1983). In the absence of such ability, it is possible only to approximate the circumstances under which causality can be observed and make informed guesses about the causal relations. Causal analysis thus has a logical component with which causal inference is justified, a methodological component that indicates how to go about approximating the unattainable ideal circumstances for observing causality, and an empirical component that provides the observational facts on which inference is supported in a particular case.

Treatment Theory Versus the Black Box

The premise of this chapter is that all three of the components of causal analysis are importantly and substantially strengthened by an explicit theory about the nature and details of the change mechanism through which the cause of interest is expected to produce the effect(s) of interest. In particular, this chapter is concerned with "treatment theory," which attempts to describe the process through which an intervention is expected to have effects on a specified target population. A closer look at the practical circumstances within which causal analysis is generally done will set the stage for this discussion.

Most situations in which intervention might be attempted can be characterized as "black boxes." Black boxes, as Ashby (1956) defined them, are organisms, devices, or situations for which inputs and outputs can be observed, but the connecting processes are not readily visible. A simple, prototypical black box model is depicted in Figure 1.1.

Black boxes are an apt depiction of many human situations in which an intervention is desirable. Through social action upon various black boxes—that is, through treatments, programs, policies, and the like—various agents seek to influence often-complex problem situations in ways that better the human condition. Within the domain of practical or applied social science, there are two types of interesting situations. In one case, the objective is to manipulate inputs, that is, provide treatments, in order to

Figure 1.1. Prototypical Black Box Model

produce beneficial outputs. The other is the case in which the goal is to identify the causes of dysfunctional outputs, such as undesirable medical, psychological, or social conditions, so that those conditions can be prevented. Methodologically, there are only two general approaches that will support reasonable causal inference. It is possible to manipulate the inputs and observe how outputs are affected, that is, an experiment can be conducted. Or an investigator can observe, but not manipulate, variations in input and attempt to relate those to variation in output—an observational or correlational approach.

In either case, the task of designing causal research is largely a matter of mapping events onto a research paradigm (Chen and Rossi, 1980). That is, the segment of reality that is of interest is mapped or coded into variables and relationships that, in turn, are operationalized as measures (observations) and procedures. In a very literal sense, the research study itself is a model or representation of what are taken to be the important features and relations of the respective reality. Moreover, much of what is meant by "validity" in research has to do with the correspondence or fit between the research representation and the substantive reality of interest (Brinberg and McGrath, 1985).

Ashby's black box provides the minimal generic specification of variables and relationships necessary for causal research. It is necessary only to identify the black box of interest (for example, a target population such as asthmatics), an input to manipulate or observe (for example, ingestion of vitamin B_6), and an outcome of interest (for example, wheezing). Proper observation of subjects' consumption of vitamin B_6 and a reasonable measure of wheezing comprise the rudiments of a study of the causal proposition that vitamin B_6 reduces wheezing in asthmatics.

Comparison of this research paradigm to the segment of reality that it maps reveals that it has simplified and abstracted that reality to a considerable extent. The typical research design does not depend on, or necessarily offer, any description of the causal process at work between the treatment and the outcome—that part is left inside the black box. Moreover, in the experimental version of the paradigm, the treatment is generally applied in molar fashion as an undifferentiated whole present with all its concomitants in one condition and absent in the other. In its minimal form, this research paradigm is almost completely an atheoretical "try this and see if it works" approach. Most treatment effectiveness research in the social sciences is in fact conducted in this minimalist form or close to it

(Lipsey and others, 1985), and the situation may not be very different in the medical sciences (Kleinman, 1986).

There can be little quarrel with this minimalist research paradigm when it is applied to relatively simple situations, such as input events that are basically indivisible molar wholes, a few well-defined outcome states, and input-output changes that are contiguous, immediate, and direct. Indeed, it is worth remembering that, in the Fisherian tradition, experimental design was invented for agricultural studies that had many of these properties. However, most causal phenomena of practical interest are more complex. They involve multidimensional interactions that often are extended over time, complex multistep causal processes in which different individuals may react differently, and uncertain and potentially wide-ranging outcomes, not all necessarily desirable.

Clearly, these more complex cases can be, and frequently are, approached in the minimalist black box paradigm. A complex and varying set of ill-defined educational activities, such as the Head Start Program, can be defined as a package, applied to a treatment group, and withheld from a control group. After a reasonable period of time, various outcomes measures can be taken to see if the groups differ. With proper research design, this approach can establish empirical, molar cause-and-effect linkages involving manipulable treatment packages. From a practical standpoint, these treatment packages provide buttons that, when pressed, produce useful effects; it may seem that little more could be desired. Press the planned parenthood button, and the birthrate goes down; press the Sesame Street button, and children's academic proficiency goes up; press the antismoking campaign button, and cancer rates decrease; and so forth. Any policymaker, human services professional, or social do-gooder would be delighted to have all of these buttons identified for practical use.

Despite the appeal of these simple cause-and-effect images, application of the molar black box research paradigm to complex phenomena often underrepresents and oversimplifies to such a degree that the results are crude and distorted depictions of the circumstances investigated. The coding of input as molar categories may obscure its multidimensional character, overlook important variability within the categories, and ignore exogenous variables that may accompany and interact with input. Treatment of the causal relationship itself as an unexamined process within the black box may make it impossible to understand how it works, what intervening or mediating variables are critical, and what interactions with subject and setting characteristics occur. On the output side, the molar black box paradigm often focuses on a narrow range of dependent variables to the neglect of unexpected side effects, the interrelationships among effects, and the timing, magnitude, and durability of those effects.

The alternative to black box research, of course, is to differentiate the research paradigm in ways that better represent the underlying complexity. Such differentiation results in a research study that more richly represents the details of the causal process of interest. Even more important, it supports the construction of differentiated concepts about the processes involved, which can lead to sophisticated causal theory instead of the simple but vague empirical facts that result from molar black box experimentation on complex causal situations. The Catch-22 for this approach is that meaningful differentiation of input, causal process, and output requires that the research begin with a conceptual or theoretical framework on which such differentiation can be based. Any approach to experimental research on treatment effectiveness other than the molar black box approach, therefore, requires the researcher to be theory-oriented. In the bootstrapping pattern so common in science, theory must play a role prior to the research, as a basis for planning, and a role after the research, as a scheme for organization and interpretation of results and as a target for revision or rejection in the face of those results.

Given the extra burden that theory orientation places on the researcher and the research process, the crucial question is, "What is gained by conducting theory-oriented treatment effectiveness research?" In basic research, this is a frivolous question, since theory building is the primary motive of the endeavor. In the practical and applied domain, it is a question that deserves thoughtful consideration. Some answers are itemized below (see also Adelman, 1986; Bickman, 1987; Chen and Rossi, 1980, 1983; Cordray and Lipsey, 1987; Hawkins, 1978; Mark, 1986; Sechrest, 1986a).

Discovery. The molar black box approach to treatment effectiveness research implicitly relies on a trial-and-error process for discovery of promising treatments. Candidate treatments may arise serendipitously, come from an atheoretical "let's try this and see if it works" experimentation, or be developed by practitioners as reflections of their intuition and experience (Campbell, 1986). The up-or-down results of molar black box tests of such treatments give little guidance about how they might be improved or where to look for better tests. At best, a trial-and-error approach is an inefficient way to discover promising treatment approaches. At worst, it floats on the surface of the target problems, testing what seems reasonable or is popular at the moment but not probing into the (possibly counterintuitive) causal heart of the matter. Theory-oriented treatment research, at least as a complement to serendipity and clinical intuition, has the advantages of supporting inferences about new treatment approaches with potential for success and providing a conceptual basis for refining and improving existing treatment.

Research Design. Somewhat paradoxically, theory orientation may have its greatest advantage in the domain of practical research design. The task of studying the effects of complex treatments on complex human beings under relatively uncontrolled field conditions is no easy matter. A theory orientation provides a framework within which the researcher can address the fundamental but vexing questions of which controls to implement, which samples to use, which measures to take, and which procedures to follow. It can help guide the research to designs that have increased probability of detecting treatment effects, permit stronger causal inference, and produce more interpretable and generalizable results. These matters are of such importance to conducting treatment effectiveness research that they are revisited in greater detail later in this chapter.

Knowledge and Application. As Aristotle says in *Metaphysics,* "What we call wisdom has to do with first causes and principles of things." He goes on to say that the masters of a craft are those who know the reasons for the things that are done, the whys and the causes. Such knowledge permits treatment to be applied in an intelligent and responsive fashion rather than in mechanical or stereotyped form. When "the why" and "the cause" are known, an approach can be adapted to varying circumstances. When only the empirical fact is known, the treatment can only be reproduced as ritual in the hope that it will have the expected effects. No matter how numerous, disjointed empirical cause-and-effect facts do not make for knowledge about treatment and the problems that treatment addresses. Knowledge, in contrast to facts, requires theory, that is, a framework of interconnected concepts that gives meaning and explanation to relevant events and supports new insights and problem-solving efforts. Theory-oriented treatment research holds out the promise of increasing knowledge in ways that build the practical science of social intervention while informing policy and practice throughout the helping disciplines.

Nature of Theory in Practical Science

Two kinds of theory are relevant to practical science: theory that models ameliorative processes, such as treatments or programs, and theory that models the processes that produce problems needing amelioration, such as personal or social dysfunctions (Chen and Rossi, 1980). It should be quite clear that these are not the same. Treatment theory deals with the change mechanism through which treatment can have effects on the problem. Problem theory deals with the natural or social causes of the problem. An understanding of how a problem comes about often suggests possible approaches to treatment, but there is no necessity for the processes that produce the problem to play a role in remedying it. A headache, for example, may be produced by tension, dilation of capillaries, and other such factors, while an effective treatment for headache may consist of an analgesic that raises pain thresholds—a connected but different causal process.

Moreover, there is a relationship between the two types of theory and the two methods for investigating causality mentioned earlier. Typically, experimental methodology is restricted to the investigation of treatment effects because it is rarely possible to manipulate directly the inputs that contribute to problem situations. Thus, treatment theory is generally more pertinent for experimental or quasi-experimental investigation than for observational or correlational investigation. The etiology of problem situations, to which problem theory applies, is more likely to be studied using correlational methods.

Although this discussion is restricted to treatment theory and the techniques used to investigate treatment effectiveness, there are strong parallels between the role of treatment theory in experimental research and the role of problem theory in correlational research. Much of what can be said about the former also applies to the latter, but no attempt is made here to be explicit about those parallels.

Treatment Theory

Treatment theory is a set of propositions regarding what goes on in the black box during the transformation of input to output, that is, how a bad situation is transformed into a better one through treatment inputs. It is a small theory attempting explanation of specific treatment processes, not a large theory of general social or biological phenomena. Appropriate elements of treatment theory include the following: (1) a problem definition that specifies what condition is treatable, for which populations, and under what circumstances, that is, a statement of boundaries that distinguishes relevant from irrelevant situations; (2) specification of the critical inputs (what is necessary, what is sufficient, and what is optimal to produce the expected effects), the interrelationships among the inputs, and the basis for judging magnitude or strength of inputs (for example, dosage levels); (3) the important steps, links, phases, or parameters of the transformation process that the treatment brings about, the intervening or mediating variables on which the process is contingent, and the crucial interactions with individual differences, timing, mode of delivery, or other relevant circumstances; and (4) specification of the expected output (nature, range, and timing of various treatment effects and side effects) and the interrelationships or contingencies among the outputs.

In addition, treatment theory might well encompass other factors (Bickman, 1987; Chen and Rossi, 1983; Finney and Moos, 1984; Rossi, 1978; Scheirer, 1987; Sechrest, 1986a). For example, there may be (1) exogenous factors, that is, contextual or environmental factors that will significantly affect treatment processes (such as facilities, training of personnel, and social conditions, which may include organizational factors, especially when treatments are embedded in broader programs); (2) implementation issues, that is, aspects of the treatment delivery system relevant to its function of providing the specified treatment; or (3) stochastic factors, that is, probabilistic disturbances of the social, treatment, and research circumstances involved in any program; background variability in events, persons, measures; and so forth.

Several caveats are in order at this point. First, it is counterproductive to approach treatment theory by holding dogmatically to a doctrine. The relationship between treatment theory and research constitutes an iterative process in which theory is subject to refinement and rejection as additional evidence edits theory and as improved theory leads to additional evidence. Second, it is not presumed that research needs to proceed on the basis of a single treatment theory; indeed, many treatment circumstances are so complex that numerous theories are equally plausible (Bickman, 1987; Gottfredson, 1984; McClintock, 1987). Different researchers may use different conceptual frameworks, and a single researcher may entertain multiple working hypotheses (Chamberlin, 1965). Finally, it is not necessary for treatment theory to be elaborate and detailed in order to be useful. It is more important for the theory to be explicit, so that its implications for research design and interpretation can be carefully considered. Relatively little is needed on this score to improve the current state of evaluation practice.

As Lipsey and others (1985) showed, over 70 percent of the studies in a representative sample of published treatment effectiveness research offered either no theory or only general statements of the program strategy or principles. Fewer than 10 percent presented any theoretical context more general than the empirical relations among the variables under investigation, that is, some integrated theory linking program elements, rationale, and treatment processes.

Sources of Treatment Theory

A major handicap for the position espoused in this chapter is the relative lack of readily available and pertinent background theory for most medical, psychological, educational, and social treatments of practical interest. In comparison with the wealth of physical and chemical theory available to an engineer, the social sciences have little to offer, and the health sciences are somewhere in between. Treatment practice, therefore, may run well ahead of treatment theory, that is, very promising treatments may be designed on the basis of the experience and intuition of practitioners with little theoretical structure. Given this state of affairs, other approaches to theory development for treatments must generally be considered. Three such approaches are as follows.

First, make what use is possible of "off-the-shelf" theory from relevant disciplines. Often this will be unsatisfactory, but it may provide a point of departure, if not a usable theoretical framework. At a minimum, previous research on the treatment of interest should be examined; or, for innovations, similar treatments should be examined and relevant concepts identified. Sometimes a theoretical perspective from a different area can be used effectively for a treatment situation. For example, Weinholtz and Friedman (1985) used small group leadership theory as a starting point to orient their study of the effectiveness of teaching by attending physicians in a medical school. A more detailed example is the extensive mapping of social learning theory onto the case of family intervention as a treatment for antisocial children that has been developed over more than a decade at the Oregon Social Learning Center (Patterson, 1986).

Second, develop theory in separate studies prior to the evaluation of the treatment or program. When possible, develop the program on the basis of prior pilot studies that differentiate and test the components of treatment. Wang and Walberg (1983) used this latter approach effectively to design and evaluate a program of "adaptive learning environments" for elementary school students. Starting with relevant theory from cognitive psychology and teaching effectiveness research, they developed, tested, and modified various program components before these components were assembled into a program model and evaluated under field conditions. More generally, this approach might begin with extensive qualitative investigation of the domain of interest to identify important factors and relationships in order both to stimulate theorizing and, more important, to ground it in detailed observation (Glaser and Strauss, 1967).

Third, draw out the theory or theories implicit in any operational program or treatment from program personnel, relevant clinical practitioners, or recipients. In recent years, a number of techniques have been developed for this task (McClintock, 1987). They range from relatively unstructured interview or interaction techniques (Gottfredson, 1984; Wholey, 1987) to very structured scaling and clustering techniques (Bougon, 1983; Trochim, 1983, 1985), with various questionnaire approaches in between (Conrad and Miller, 1987). For example, Gottfredson (1984) described the "program development evaluation approach" in which researchers use organizational development techniques to collaborate with program personnel in identifying problems, setting goals, deriving action theories, and evaluating interventions in an iterative cycle aimed at producing stronger programs and better intervention theory.

Obviously, these approaches are not mutually exclusive, and most require that researchers do a great deal of the theory synthesizing themselves. This demanding task requires, at a minimum, that the researchers have in mind a variety of possible formats within which to express theoretical perspectives on a treatment. It may be instructive to review some of the formats more likely to be appropriate (Lipsey and Pollard, 1989).

Basic Two-Step. The minimal improvement that a researcher might make in a black box representation of the treatment process is to specify the key intervening variables that connect treatment with outcome, thereby defining a simple two-step treatment theory. One step represents the assumption that program operations actually affect the intervening variables; the other step represents the assumption that a change in the identified intervening variables will result in a change in the target outcome variables. For example, Chandler (1973) identified social egocentrism as an important mediating factor in juvenile delinquency and designed an intervention based on the training of role-taking skills. The evaluation results showed an increase in role-taking ability, the mediating variable, and a corresponding decrease in delinquency.

Causal Diagram. A familiar way to depict causal processes is through a causal diagram that identifies important variables (as boxes or labels) and their causal influences (as arrows) on one another. The causal diagram may be an informal sketch of the variables identified and relationships hypothesized, or it may be a more carefully defined "model" for input into structural equation analysis (Judd and Kenny, 1981). Rossi, Berk, and Lenihan (1980) used this approach to model the effects of paying unemployment benefits to released felons. This format highlighted the possibility of opposing causal processes: decreased economic hardship with potential for lowering criminal activity versus work disincentive effects with potential for raising it. Judd and Kenny (1981) offered a simpler example in their illustration of the causal links in the Stanford Heart Disease Prevention Project. Their causal analysis hypothesized that the treatment (mass media and personal instruction) would affect knowledge about dietary factors associated with heart disease risk, which in turn would lead to changes in dietary practices that would yield changes in levels of serum cholesterol and triglyceride in the blood.

Stage-State Analysis. Many program and treatment processes can be conceptualized most easily in terms of the various stages and states through which clients progress—and occasionally regress—under the influence of treatment (Brownell, Marlatt, Lichtenstein, and Wilson, 1986). Where the causal diagram works with variables and causal arrows, the stage-state analysis works with categories and transition probabilities (Runyan, 1980). Caplan's (1968) analysis of the interaction of juveniles with street gang workers demonstrates the basic framework. Caplan classified the progress of each juvenile into eight stages. Early stages were related to the youth's participation in program activities; later stages represented the therapeutic relationship with the counselor and, finally, the autonomy of changed behavior. For each stage, a juvenile could be in one of four states: not yet at the stage, at the stage, regressed from the stage to an earlier stage, or passed beyond the stage. With this framework, Caplan was able to categorize the developmental path of each juvenile through the program and produce insights into many aspects of the treatment process.

A similar approach focusing more on organizational categories and statuses was taken by Taber and Poertner (1981) in a study of a large child care system. They were able to show that changed client status was more a function of the organization than of the behavior of either the client or the treatment professional.

Substantive Model. Treatment processes that deal with physical or biological mechanisms often can be modeled in substantive terms. That is, a specific physical or physiological mechanism is described in terms of its components and processes, and the treatment effects are mapped onto that mechanism. This is the type of theory that describes how a clock works, how hormones affect eating behavior, and how dialysis works for victims of kidney failure.

Role of Theory in Method

The foregoing has made a general case for the use of theory in treatment effectiveness research, described what is meant by theory, and provided guidance on how to develop theory. The stage is set for the major focus of this chapter: detailed consideration of the role of theory in treatment evaluation methodology. To provide an organizational framework for discussion, this topic is considered in relation to each of four crucial issues in treatment effectiveness research.

First, the research design must be based on relevant constructs and variables. Second, the important outcomes that occur subsequent to treatment must be detected. Third, those outcomes must be attributable to the treatment. Fourth, the overall pattern of results must be interpretable and have practical implications.

The central argument developed here is that consideration of each of these issues is substantially aided by treatment theory. Advice is offered on the effective use of treatment theory as a methodological tool. Of particular interest is the important role of theory in quasi-experimental research, where the lack of controls increases the ambiguity of the results.

Problem Specification. Nothing improves research design so much as having a clear idea about what is being investigated. An important function of theory in research design is to help researchers ensure that they are playing in the right ballpark to begin with, that is, to help them avoid studying the wrong thing. In the planning stages, all research must begin with a statement of the research question to be investigated and a corresponding identification of the relevant constructs and issues. On this basis, the methodological approach is chosen (for example, experimental, correlational, or descriptive), variables are specified and operationalized, and research procedures are planned. The role of theory in identifying the constructs and relationships relevant to a research problem can be illustrated by examining four aspects of research planning.

Global Plausibility. As Chen and Rossi (1983) point out, many treatments and programs are simply not plausible, either from a common-sense standpoint or on the basis of existing knowledge. They give the example of the 1968 Federal Firearms Regulation Act, which assumed, implausibly, that criminals obtain their guns from commercial dealers, that dealers can recognize prohibited persons who attempt a purchase, and that registration records can easily be used to trace gun ownership. The research frame for implausible treatments should of necessity be different from that for plausible treatments. Given the likelihood that the treatment will prove ineffective, the research should make special effort to identify faulty assumptions and document their deficiencies. Potentially, it would be even more useful to develop an alternate treatment theory applicable to the same context and incorporate an assessment of its assumptions into the research.

Even when a treatment is plausible, the research can benefit from an application of alternate theoretical perspectives to the treatment circumstances in an effort to identify important constructs. For example, psychotherapy could be examined in terms of the constructs salient in the clinical literature and also in terms of persuasion or attitude change processes that might highlight a different set of constructs (see McClintock, 1987, for other examples of multiple perspectives).

Independent-Variable Issues. The researcher must decide how to represent the treatment—that is, the independent variable—in the research. The conventional approach is to encode only one aspect of treatment, whether or not it was present as a molar whole. However, in bringing a theoretical analysis to the treatment, one can reveal numerous other aspects that may be worth considering, especially in the case of complex treatments. For example, it will almost always be relevant to have some idea of the continuum of strength of treatment (Sechrest and others, 1979), in other words, the dosage level at which the treatment is implemented. If treatment strength is low relative to the target problem, little in the way of positive results can be expected. A reasonable approach may be a parametric study in which various dosage levels are implemented and compared. This may be a straightforward approach with pharmaceutical treatments, where the dosage continuum is largely a matter of quantity and frequency, but it may require careful analysis in other contexts. What, for example, is the dosage continuum for medical instruction, physical therapy, family planning counseling, or psychotherapy (Howard, Kopta, Krause, and Orlinsky, 1986)? For complex treatments, it may be questionable whether a single dimension of treatment strength is adequate to represent the treatment construct. Datta (1976) suggests that it may be necessary to use an explicitly multidimensional representation of the treatment. For example, it may be possible to break the treatment down into activities or components (Bickman, 1985) in order to consider their individual contributions to treatment effects and their interactions with each other.

A further complication is that with all but the simplest treatments there is considerable potential for the effects of treatment to interact with characteristics of the treatment delivery system (Rossi, 1978), such as the resources available and the skill and motivation of staff. To represent this situation, the researcher needs a clear distinction between the delivery system and the treatment, as well as an analysis of where they interact. One simple construct frequently applicable to the delivery system is its integrity (Yeaton and Sechrest, 1981), that is, the extent to which the treatment plan is implemented. A strong treatment poorly implemented cannot be expected to have effects, but this interaction will not be apparent to the researcher who does not distinguish between treatment strength and treatment integrity.

Datta (1976) suggests various ways of handling the implementation issue, such as restricting the research to well-implemented treatments, blocking different implementation levels together so that differences among levels can be compared, and defining a measurable implementation continuum that can be used as a variable in the analysis. In all cases, some measure or index of implementation is required, which necessitates identification of the constructs along which important variation in implementation can take place (Rezmovic, 1984; Scheirer and Rezmovic, 1983).

Subject Issues. Without clear specification of the problem that the treatment is expected to remedy and, more particular, the target population, treatment effectiveness research has considerable potential for misrepresentation. Target groups that do not have the problem or are not at risk for the problem obviously cannot be helped by treatment, no matter how effective. The task of defining the target population is not problematic in cases where there are relatively straightforward, observable, and unambiguous symptoms to provide criteria. In other cases, however, adequate definition requires a framework of concepts about the nature of the problem and its observable manifestation in the target population.

Consider, for example, juvenile delinquents as a target population for remedial treatment. At first blush, it would seem very easy to define this group. Usually, they are identified according to their arrest records. It is now known, however, that most juveniles who are arrested by the police are not chronic delinquents and, furthermore, that most chronic delinquents are not arrested by the police (Dunford and Elliott, 1984; Elliott, Dunford, and Huizinga, 1986). Therefore, researchers who are studying treatments for delinquency face a considerable challenge in specifying the symptoms or indicators that identify the population for whom treatment is appropriate. Without some prior understanding and a framework of appropriate constructs, such identification may be virtually impossible (Loeber and Stouthamer-Loeber, 1987).

Given a definition of the target population, another set of issues comes into play. Can that population be expected to be homogeneous with regard to characteristics that interact with treatment effectiveness? Some treatments, like being hit on the head with a baseball bat, affect everyone about the same. Others, like psychotherapy, are apt to have varying effects depending on the circumstances and characteristics of each recipient. In the latter cases, there are a variety of subpopulations for whom treatment-outcome relationships may differ. Failure to distinguish among them misrepresents treatment effects and muddies an understanding of the nature of treatment benefits. To find such patterns of differential response, measures must be included for those subject characteristics likely to interact with treatment. This, in turn, requires a conceptual framework within which such relations can be hypothesized. Miller (1985) illustrates such a framework with his thorough review of the important role of motivational variables in treatment entry, compliance, and outcome for alcoholics and other addicts. For these populations, resistance to treatment plays a major role in the relationship between program inputs and outputs (Snowden, 1984); failure to account for this treatment resistance leads to ambiguous research results, whatever the outcome.

Dependent-Variable Issues. Chen and Rossi (1980) argue that every program disturbs the targeted social system to some extent and thus has some effects, though possibly trivial. The challenge for evaluation research is to know which effects are important and to be able to detect them. Perhaps the most important, yet most neglected, function of theory in treatment research is its capacity to aid the researcher in specifying the constructs or variables on which change can reasonably be expected as a result of a given treatment, that is, specification of which behaviors, states, conditions, and so forth are likely to be affected. Without this specification, there is little basis for selection of outcomes measures and little assurance that the measures selected are appropriate. Even a researcher who elects to proceed on a black box basis with regard to treatment inputs needs specification of the expected outcomes. Independent variables can be manipulated, permitting the researcher some control even without a close understanding of the nature of the variables. Dependent variables, however, must be anticipated and measured, which inescapably requires specification of the constructs to be represented in the measures.

There are at least three aspects of the specification of outcome variables, each requiring some a priori theory, even if only at the level of hunches and hypotheses. However, the better the theory, the better is the resulting specification of expected outcomes. First, a researcher must know what construct domains are subject to change as a result of a given treatment (which behaviors, states, conditions, and so on are likely to be affected). The more complex the treatment program, the more uncertainty there is about the range and nature of possible outcomes. As has been widely noted, the official statements of treatment goals are typically too vague to provide adequate research guidance or, at best, are limited to comments about a select few target benefits expected. Other possible outcomes, such as adverse side effects or unintended benefits, are rarely anticipated in official program goals (or may be specifically excluded; see O'Sullivan, Burleson, and Lamb, 1985, on evaluation of cutbacks in renal dialysis services). While a broad, unconstrained search for such unintended effects (for example, the "goal-free evaluation" of Scriven, 1974) can be advocated, the possibilities are limitless, and practicality requires that the domain be narrowed in some reasonable manner, for example, on the basis of some treatment theory that provides guidance (Sherrill, 1984).

Although important, identification of the construct domains within which effects are considered possible only amounts to development of a set of labels or variable names. A crucial and widely underappreciated next step is specification of the operational details of the measures that will represent those constructs in the research design. This step requires very close specification of the nature of expected effects, and it relies heavily on some conceptual framework, whether implicit or, far better, explicit. The following examples illustrate the nature of the issues at this stage of research.

One neglected aspect in the selection of operational measures is the extent to which measures that appear to be only slightly different can yield different results. Of necessity, the researcher must be clear about which outcome aspect is most important to measure. Consider, for example, a simple learning outcome of an education intervention. Are the effects to be manifest primarily as knowledge (in other words, operationally, the student can explain the subject matter), as application (the student can appropriately apply knowledge to new situations), or as recognition (the student recognizes correct answers)? Measures based on these different operationalizations will be less than perfectly correlated and may yield different results.

Datta (1976) cites an evaluation in which an expected program outcome was greater "career maturity." "Career attitude" was the measure used, and according to the test developer, it was not synonymous with "career maturity." This type of slippage is all too common in evaluation research.

Other operational details of outcome measures also need to be informed by a theory of expected effects. For example, Shapiro (1984b) raises the issue of the distribution of effects. As Shapiro points out, in terms of the expected effect of an education program, there is a great deal of difference among raising the achievement level of every recipient, raising the level of those initially lowest and thus most disadvantaged, and decreasing the discrepancies between the most advantaged and the least advantaged.

The timing of measures is also important. Many studies measure dependent variables at the conclusion of treatment with perhaps one follow-up. This approach implies a model in which effects have an abrupt onset and peak immediately after treatment, but other models of effects are clearly possible. For example, effects could peak early in treatment and then decline, or there could be large "sleeper" effects, little effects at the end of treatment but much larger effects later. Also, there might be different timing for different outcome variables, with some effects most pronounced immediately after treatment and others at some later time. The choice of appropriate times for outcomes measurement requires an explicit and well-justified model of the nature of the expected effects and the points at which they are expected to appear. In the absence of such a model, it is quite possible that even with careful research, an investigator will fail to detect important treatment effects simply by looking in the wrong place at the wrong time.

A final issue involves knowing what constitutes a meaningful outcome once adequate measurement has been operationalized. Here, at least two facets of the problem require some underlying framework or theory. First, the centrality of the result (Datta, 1976) is at issue. Some outcomes are more important than others, and good research should reflect a clear comprehension of which is which. Second, the practical significance of any effect found is at issue, that is, the size of effect that would be meaningful in the context of the treatment and target problem.

It is widely acknowledged that an effect can be statistically significant but not practically significant (the reverse is also possible, of course). Identification of appropriate criteria for judging practical significance requires some concept of the problem situation (Datta, 1980; Sechrest and Yeaton, 1981). For example, the effects of remedial programs might be judged according to the extent to which they closed the gap between the disadvantaged and the "normal" population. Alternatively, some quality-of-life framework might be invoked in which posttreatment conditions would be compared with a minimal set of standards for personal functioning (Baker and Intagliata, 1982). Without such a framework, measured outcomes remain at the operational and statistical level and cannot be retranslated into their implications for the original constructs of interest in the treatment or problem context.

Statistical Detection of Effects. After the treatment, subjects, and outcomes measures are specified, attention is directed to the ability of the planned research to detect whatever treatment effects are present. It is increasingly clear that a major shortcoming of much practical treatment research is inadequate statistical power that yields null results even when the treatment is genuinely effective (Cohen, 1982; Lipsey and others, 1985; Rossi and Wright, 1984; Schneider and Darcy, 1984). A low probability of detecting treatment effects originates in a combination of common circumstances. Often there are limited numbers of subjects available for research, and, among those who do participate, attrition rates can be high. In addition, under field conditions, treatment may be implemented inconsistently or at reduced strength, and data collection and measurement may be subject to various disturbances that lower reliability (Boruch and Gomez, 1977; Lipsey, 1983).

Statistical power is a function of the effect size to be detected, the sample size, the alpha level set by the researcher (conventionally, $p < .05$), and the type of statistical test employed. The last two factors offer limited opportunity for improvement. Of course, the most straightforward approach to increasing statistical power is to use larger samples. Since it is often not possible to obtain the optimal number of subjects under practical conditions, researchers may sweep the power issue under the rug, assuming that there is nothing else to be done. In fact, there are effective strategies available for increasing statistical power without necessarily increasing sample size (Lipsey, 1990). However, many of these strategies depend on assumptions about the treatment process and the subjects' reactions to it.

If the number of subjects is constrained, the only remaining parameter is effect size. Although effect size (always some variation on percentage of dependent-variable variance accounted for by the independent variable) may appear to be a fixed value for a given treatment or research context, many of the factors that determine effect size can be constructively influenced by the researcher (Sechrest and Yeaton, 1982). To illustrate this point, two factors that greatly influence effect size are considered: the sensitivity of the dependent measures to the treatment effect and the extent to which the "error" variance on the dependent variable can be controlled.

Measurement Sensitivity. Outcomes measures that are responsive to treatment-induced change yield comparatively large effects and, hence, increased statistical power. The sensitivity of a dependent measure is a function of a number of factors, including construct validity, ceiling and floor effects, and the units in which it is scaled. Most important, measurement sensitivity is a matter of how closely the measure is keyed to the specific nature of the change expected. At issue in the measurement response to change is whether the measure is to be oriented to the overall level of performance after treatment or to the amount of change in performance occurring over the pretreatment to posttreatment interval.

For example, suppose the treatment of interest is elementary school arithmetic instruction, in particular, the teaching of fractions. The effects of such teaching could be measured in two different ways. In one approach, the students would be given a mathematics achievement test appropriate to their grade level. If they have received effective instruction, their scores should increase on such a test. Note, however, that the increase will be incremental, and many other factors, including natural aptitude and prior learning, also will be reflected in the scores. The net result is that the difference between a group receiving instruction and a group that does not will be only a small portion of the full range of scores.

The second approach is more similar to what the teacher is likely to do, that is, give a test on fractions. A test that is carefully focused on the content of the relevant instructional domain can be expected to be much more responsive to instructional effects. It is quite possible that all students in a group not receiving instruction would score virtually zero on such a test, while all those with instruction would score virtually 100 percent. In this case, the group difference is not incremental but represents nearly the full range of scores on the measure. This example contrasts psychometric measures with criterion-referenced measures (Carver, 1974), but the issue is somewhat more general. Any treatment effect can be looked at in terms of the specific changes that are expected to take place or in terms of the broader content or performance domain within which the changes are to occur. A measure focused on the changes will generally show considerably larger effects than will a measure focused on the broader domain. Selection of a measure without consideration of this issue can greatly affect the research outcome. When the early Head Start researchers expected cognitive gains in target children and, largely for convenience, selected intelligence quotient (IQ) measures (which, by definition, are not supposed to change), they almost guaranteed that negligible effects would be found. When a program to decrease aggressive behavior among adolescents uses police arrest rates as a dependent variable, a similar choice is made (Lipsey, 1983).

Though measurement sensitivity is clearly important to the ability of treatment research to detect effects, this issue cannot be approached without at least rudimentary treatment theory. The selection of measures focused on the specific changes expected from treatment requires a relatively detailed model of just what change process the treatment induces. Similarly, selection of appropriate measures for the broader domain within which change takes place also requires careful clarification of the nature of that domain and its relevance as an arena for treatment effects.

Error Control. The effect size parameter in statistical power compares the difference between treatment and control group means to the within-groups variability. Any procedure that reduces the within-groups variability will increase effect size and, therefore, statistical power. Thus, a given difference between a treatment and a control group will be statistically significant if the variance within the groups on the pertinent measure is sufficiently small, and insignificant if that variance is sufficiently large.

The source of variation in dependent variables is of interest to the researcher who is attempting to improve statistical power. The potential sources are numerous; indeed, any factor that differentially affects the scores across subjects contributes to this variance. Familiar sources of this so-called error variance that are at least partially under the researcher's control include the reliability of the measures used, the consistency of the experimental procedures, and the subject-sampling strategies. (While important, the rationale for these factors is drawn almost entirely from concepts of statistical theory and research design that cannot be pursued here.) At least three other factors that are relevant to error variance can be used effectively only when guided by treatment theory. One such factor is the natural heterogeneity of subjects on the dependent variables prior to treatment, that is, the different baseline values from which different subjects begin. Such differences become part of the error term for statistical significance testing. If subjects are relatively homogeneous, a smaller difference between treatment and control group is required for statistical significance. One straightforward approach to controlling for this source of variance is to administer pretests on the variables of interest, which are then entered as covariates or blocking factors in the analysis of posttest values. Pretests are not always feasible, however, and other covariates may be used (for example, sex, age, socioeconomic status, and IQ). Such covariates are effective only to the extent that they are related to the dependent variables of interest. The selection of appropriate covariates requires an understanding of the nature of the dependent variables and the pattern of relationships in which they are involved for the target population; these are elements of what is called treatment theory. IQ, for example, is generally a good stand-in variable for initial differences on academic achievement tests because of its theoretical and empirical links with that performance domain.

A similar situation occurs when there is likelihood of differential subject response to treatment, that is, when treatment does not increase every subject's score by a constant increment. If some subjects react more strongly than others on the dependent-variable dimensions, that variability will inflate the value of the error term and reduce the overall treatment-control contrast to an average that obscures the uneven effects of treatment on different subjects. The only way to distinguish such variability from other sources of error so that it can be removed from the analysis is by identifying those subject variables that are related to the extent of response to treatment and including them in the statistical model as covariates or blocking factors that interact with the treatment-outcome relationship. For example, in a study of brief inpatient psychiatric treatment, Smith, Cardillo, and Choate (1984) found that the outcome for male veterans had a complex relationship to age: Patients treated during adult developmental transition periods improved the most.

The effects of differential response to treatment on ability to detect treatment effects were shown in even more striking form by Crano and Messe (1985). When they applied standard analytical techniques to data from a complex energy conservation intervention, they found no effects. A refined analysis, however, showed that the treatment had considerable impact on those whose comprehension of the treatment contingencies was high, but this effect was lost when all subjects were analyzed together.

Another source of differential subject response is differential treatment. That is, the treatment may lack integrity in that some subjects receive more or less of the treatment, larger or smaller doses, longer or shorter periods of contact, and so on and show proportionately larger or smaller effects. Variability in treatment delivery generally produces variability in the response to treatment. Such variability shows up in the error terms against which the treatment effects are tested.

Degradation of treatment delivery also has the potential of so diluting treatment overall that the main effect is attenuated. Ideally, treatments would be tested under conditions of high strength and integrity in which little variation occurs. For complex treatments, especially when subjects are volunteers, it is often difficult to maintain a constant dose. If the researcher has a workable notion of the important dimensions of treatment strength and integrity, those dimensions can be measured separately and be included in the analysis with the same effect of reducing error variance as a covariate predicting differential subject response. In this case, it is the treatment delivery that is being modeled and not other bases for the subject response. For example, Cook and Poole (1982) demonstrated the increase in statistical power that resulted in an evaluation of a nutrition supplementation program when data on the level of treatment implementation were included directly in the analysis (but see Mark, 1983, for a pertinent caution). The gain in power was attained by the simple technique of using an independent variable to represent treatment as a continuum of degrees rather than as a dichotomy crudely contrasting treatment versus no treatment (see Johnston, Ettema, and Davidson, 1980, for a similar approach).

Refined effect measurement and statistical error control can have appreciable influence on the effect size function in experimental research and a corresponding influence on the statistical power of the design, that is, its ability to detect treatment effects. The use of such refined techniques is, of necessity, dependent on a good understanding of practical statistical theory. In many cases, however, it is equally dependent on a good understanding of treatment processes and the factors with which they interact.

Causal Attribution of Effects

In addition to constructs and measures that reasonably represent the circumstances of interest and sufficient statistical power to detect expected treatment effects, treatment research also must permit whatever effects are found to be attributed to the treatment rather than to some confounding exogenous factor. In the Campbellian framework, this is an issue of internal validity—the ability of the design to discount various rival explanations for apparent treatment effects (Campbell and Stanley, 1966; Cook and Campbell, 1979). Here, the role of theory is especially important; and the more threats to internal validity there are, the more important treatment theory becomes. The contemporary view of quasi experimentation is that it is more a system of logic than a set of techniques (Trochim, 1986a). The terms and the grounds of that logic depend crucially on the articulation of appropriate treatment theory.

As a practical matter, a causal claim is usually justified on the basis of two sets of criteria. First, researchers rely on what Einhorn and Hogarth (1986) call "cues-to-causality," in particular, temporal order (the candidate cause should precede the effect), covariation (changes in the cause should be accompanied by changes in the effect), contiguity (cause and effect should be adjacent in time and space), and congruity (there should be proportionality between the nature and magnitude of the cause and the effect). Second, plausible alternative causes of the effect must be ruled out. This concept is the familiar notion from the Campbellian tradition of quasi experimentation in which various "threats to internal validity" can be enumerated and, in valid design, can be countered item by item. For example, this approach requires a demonstration that differences between treatment and control groups after treatment cannot be accounted for by differences that were present before treatment.

In a randomized experiment conducted in the laboratory, precedence of cause and contiguity of cause and effect are established directly by manipulation of experimental conditions. Covariation and usually congruity are demonstrated when differences in the dependent variables are found for the different experimental groups. Other possible causes can be ruled out in primarily two ways.

First, the random assignment of subjects to experimental conditions provides statistical (probabilistic) assurance that there are no initial differences that could reappear in dependent measures as apparent treatment effects. However, after assignment to conditions, randomization does not exclude variables other than treatment from affecting the dependent variables of interest. Where little time elapses between assignment to conditions, treatment, and dependent-variable measurement, there is little opportunity for other influences to intrude. More generally, however, other influences are ruled out through experimental control of the circumstances. That is, between the point of assignment to groups and the measurement of dependent variables, the experimenter strives to keep the circumstances constant and comparable among experimental conditions in every relevant particular except for the treatment manipulation itself.

Nonexperimental or quasi-experimental designs for investigating treatment effects generally follow the same pattern as true experiments with the exception of randomized assignment of subjects to conditions. Thus, such designs typically provide similar evidence on the criteria of precedence of cause, contiguity, covariation, and congruity, but they allow for the possibility of initial differences among experimental groups that may rival the treatment manipulation as explanations for apparent effects.

The task of designing experimental research that results in evidence that meets the criteria for causal inference is not particularly problematic in cases where the events of interest are readily visible and immediate and where they occur within a well-understood context. To use the standard example, elaborate logic and experimental controls are not needed to conclude that the erosion of an iron bar is caused by the acid in which it is immersed. Precedence of cause, contiguity, covariation, and congruity are established by immediate perception, and everyday knowledge of the characteristics of iron bars indicates the improbability that something else in the context makes them dissolve.

Causal inference becomes much more difficult when the key events are less visible and immediate, familiarity with the factors that commonly cause change in the context is lacking, or it is clear that the effects of interest can be caused by any of a large number of factors in that context. Unfortunately, it is these more difficult inferential circumstances that generally apply to investigation of medical, psychological, educational, and social treatments. For example, psychotherapy as a treatment for depression occurs over an extended time, on more than one occasion, with results that may not appear immediately or primarily on the treatment site and may be incremental and cumulative rather than sudden and dramatic. Moreover, the effects of interest—positive mood changes, improved social functioning, and the like—are commonplace, complex, and not well understood, and they can be brought about by a host of everyday circumstances and life events other than psychotherapy.

Under such circumstances, both sets of criteria for causal inference present problems. Although research may provide evidence for the temporal precedence of cause and for covariation between cause and effect, both contiguity and congruity may be low. That is, effects will not necessarily closely follow purported causes or occur in the same settings, and their form and magnitude may bear no readily visible relation to the form and magnitude of treatment. As for ruling out rival causes, degradations to randomization or the inability to randomize at all, lack of experimental control between treatment administration and measurement of dependent variables, and the typically large number of other possible causes of the effects of interest all undermine the attempt to demonstrate that the treatment is the only plausible source of any effects found.

Good treatment theory can shore up causal inference in cases where method and circumstance result in an insufficient demonstration of causal cues or the implausibility of rival explanations. The following sections examine the roles that theory can play in augmenting cues-to-causality and eliminating rival explanations.

Cues-to-Causality. Where the purported effect comes some time after administration of the causal event, as in the effects of psychotherapy, or is not proportionate or similar to the cause, as in the effects of radiation, the causal claim is weakened by the lack of any obvious connection between cause and effect. If such a connection can be demonstrated, the causal inference gains strength. Good treatment theory provides that linkage. Treatment theory elucidates the causal chain that carries the action of the treatment through to the otherwise remote effect. If the transmission of the cause through the intermediate links can be demonstrated—for instance, by measurement of change in intervening variables—the causal inference is strengthened. Thus, the causal link between cigarette smoking and lung cancer is made more plausible by the demonstration of the presence of carcinogens in the smoke, by the mechanical connection between smoke particles and lung tissue, and by the demonstration of physiological changes in the lungs of laboratory animals exposed to heavy smoke. The causal link between fat in the diet and cancer of the colon, on the other hand, is considerably weaker due to the lack of a known mechanism through which it might work or a demonstration of the crucial intervening links.

Thus, where there is a long or complex causal chain between the commencement of the treatment and the appearance of the outcome, treatment theory that specifies the intermediate stages in the causal sequence can have a particularly persuasive role in connecting treatment with the observed effects. Research that measures those intermediate stages at the appropriate times and shows the expected state in the treatment group and the absence of that state in the control group at each stage presents a very convincing case that it was the treatment process and not something else that eventually produced the outcome of interest.

As Sechrest (1986b) and Trochim (1986b) have observed, it is difficult to find plausible rival explanations for complex theory-based predictions that are confirmed. To be effective, however, such predictions must specify outcomes in some detail (Judd and Kenny, 1981; Rosen and Proctor, 1978); a complex prediction that only implies that the treatment group will outperform the control group would not be convincing. When a treatment process is well understood, it has a characteristic modus operandi (MO) (Scriven, 1974) that can be observed by an astute researcher. Evidence of that MO in the treatment condition and a corresponding lack of that MO in the control condition strengthen the causal inference connecting treatment with outcome.

As Cordray (1986) has emphasized, it is necessary to "rule in" the treatment as a plausible cause to strengthen causal inference in these circumstances. Where the plausibility of the treatment as a cause is very high, as in the example of acid and iron given earlier, other explanations have proportionately more difficulty competing. Conversely, if the treatment is not plausible, even when supported by the research results, other explanations remain credible. Imagine a carefully randomized experiment in which subjects' names, unbeknownst to them, were engraved on iron bars, some of which were subsequently dissolved in acid. Suppose further that those subjects whose bars were dissolved had higher frequencies of accidents in the following six weeks than those whose iron bars were left intact. While there might be no doubt about the validity of the methodology in this experiment, there would almost certainly be questions about the causal attribution. In the absence of a plausible mechanism by which this ferric voodoo might effect accidental events, the empirical evidence would have to be overwhelming before a causal relationship would be accepted.

The act of ruling the treatment in as an explanation for effects has at least one other important facet: knowledge that the treatment was, in fact, administered to the treatment group and not to the control group. This might appear to be an empirical issue, but closer inspection reveals that it is theory-laden. This judgment requires a definite conception of what constitutes treatment and, often equally important, what does not. Where any variation is possible (as is often the case in applied contexts), the judgment requires knowledge of which aspects of the treatment are crucial, that is, which are the active ingredients, which variations on the treatment are considered sufficient to have effects, and so forth. These matters have as much to do with the conception of the treatment as with its operational reality and thus require at least some minimal theoretical framework.

Elimination of Rival Explanations. The ruling out of rival explanations for effects that covary with treatment is partly a matter of evidence and partly a matter of analysis and judgment. It requires identifying rivals, judging their plausibility, and, if plausible, determining what evidence bears on them (Cordray, 1986; Platt, 1964). This endeavor depends on close knowledge of the research circumstances, including the nature of the treatment process and specific context-bound arguments regarding the nature and plausibility of rival explanations. The more explicit and systematic that knowledge, the stronger are the resulting arguments. At this juncture, a differentiated program theory aids considerably in supporting causal inference in treatment research.

At a minimum, a researcher needs sufficient theory to rule out the possibility of spurious results stemming from gross violation of the assumptions of the statistical model within which covariation is analyzed. Some of those assumptions stipulate a particular form of the underlying causal processes (especially for the complex multivariate statistical analysis often required in applied treatment research). For example, relationships are customarily assumed to be linear and recursive (that is, unidirectional causality), and treatment effects are generally assumed to be additive. Therefore, the responsible researcher must postulate or demonstrate the form of certain crucial features of the causal process in order to ensure proper fit of the statistical model—a minimal but essential use of treatment theory.

Treatment theory also plays a role in examining plausible rival explanations that have to do with the initial configuration of experimental groups. In quasi-experimental designs for which there are initial group differences, those differences can only be ruled out as sources of outcome effects if their contribution to the outcome is separately accounted for prior to assessment of treatment effects. In practice, this means developing a statistical model that accounts for the differential selection of subjects into experimental groups, specifies all of the relevant variables on which the groups differ, or depicts the change or growth process that occurs between the point of group assignment and the point at which outcome is assessed (Reichardt, 1979). Given such a model and appropriate measures for the variables that it specifies, statistical adjustments may be possible that will remove the effects of initial differences from the outcome measures. The catch in this procedure is that the models must be well specified (they must contain all the relevant variables) before the procedure is trustworthy (Reichardt and Gollob, 1986). Clearly, identification of the relevant variables can occur only in situations in which the treatment process, including selection for treatment and the interaction of treatment with subject characteristics, is well understood or can be defensibly hypothesized in some detail.

A related matter has to do with "unbundling" of the treatment. Treatment as operationally applied is always a bundle of various components, some having to do with the treatment concept and others having to do with the delivery system, treatment context, and so forth. The result is that there are always rival explanations for apparent treatment effects among the concomitants of treatment. The most famous of these concomitants is the Hawthorne effect, the reaction that subjects have to the knowledge that they are the treatment group in an experiment. In order to rule out treatment concomitants as an explanation for effects, one must demonstrate that the concomitants alone are not sufficient to produce the same effects (for example, via use of a placebo control). This requires a careful analysis of the treatment bundle to distinguish the "real" treatment ingredients from the associated concomitants, a process greatly dependent on a clear conceptualization of the nature of the treatment.

Consider, for example, the continuing controversy over the nature of placebo effects in psychotherapy research. When treatment is conceptualized within the chemotherapy paradigm, where only physical and chemical manipulations count as treatment, placebo effects are artifacts to be controlled. Within the social-psychological paradigm, where communication, interaction, and suggestion are all legitimate treatment elements, placebo effects are important parts of the treatment process (Wilkins, 1986).

Theory also can be helpful, even essential, in ruling out rival explanations that have to do with differential experiences of the treatment group and the control group (other than the treatment itself) after the experiment is launched. For example, communication between the groups may contaminate the comparison, distinctive experiences of one group may alter its responses, or measurement procedures may be changed (Cook and Campbell, 1979). In order to counter such rivals, the researcher must demonstrate that either (1) nothing happened, that is, there was no differential experience other than the treatment itself, or (2) if something did happen, it did not affect the outcome, at least not enough to account for the results. A good understanding of the treatment process helps the researcher to plan studies that anticipate extraneous events that could mimic treatment effects.

For example, Kutchinsky's (1973) classic quasi-experimental analysis of the effect of the liberalization of Danish pornography laws on the incidence of sex crimes worked from a model that connected the type of offender psychology and the likely effect of pornography on the behavior of different offenders, the attitudes of potential victims toward different types of offenses and their propensity to report those offenses, and the attitudes of the police to whom offenses were reported. This model enabled identification of a number of rival explanations for the decrease in recorded offenses and collection of evidence that permitted a judgment on the plausibility of each of those rivals.

Before we leave the topic of causal inference in treatment research, a brief discussion is needed about the ubiquitous problem of subject attrition. With treatments mounted in the field using volunteer subjects—especially complex, long-term treatments—it is almost inevitable that some subjects will drop out or be otherwise unavailable at crucial data collection points (for example, Shapiro, 1984a). Even worse, subjects may cross over from one experimental group to another (Yeaton, Wortman, and Langberg, 1983). The results can be devastating to the integrity of the research design. A carefully randomized design "goes quasi" (becomes a nonequivalent comparison design) the moment there is subject attrition. In such cases, differential attrition—subjects with different characteristics dropping from the treatment versus the control group—provides a rival explanation for whatever effects are found on outcomes measures. There is no ready solution for this vexing problem.

The best that can be done to rule out differential attrition as an explanation for experimental results is to demonstrate that it did not really occur by showing that there were no differences in relevant characteristics between those who remained in the treatment group and those who remained in the control group (St. Pierre and Proper, 1978). Such a demonstration requires identification of the "relevant" characteristics and proper measurement prior to attrition. A relevant characteristic is one that interacts with the treatment process, a matter that should be specified in a good treatment theory.

Where there is differential attrition, the researcher must attempt to adjust for it, as for initial selection differences, so that it cannot account for the effects found. Such adjustments (for example, via analysis of covariance or structural equations) also require specification of the characteristics of subjects that are likely to interact with treatment or, alternatively, that are likely to motivate their attrition from treatment (Rindskopf, 1986). Again, the net result is that the researcher cannot deal effectively with the attrition problem without a good set of hypotheses about the interaction between subjects and treatment conditions.

Interpretation of Results

In practical treatment research, findings in and of themselves often have little value. Instead, their meaning and implications are what matter (Datta, 1980). The interpretation of results is an essential part of the research, and in this phase too treatment theory can play an important role. Two distinctly different cases are considered here: one in which the research produced null results (no evidence of beneficial treatment effects) and another in which the research produced positive results indicating apparent treatment success.

Null results from treatment effectiveness research are distressingly common (Lipsey and others, 1985; Rossi and Wright, 1984) and inevitably raise more questions than they answer. Treatments are not generally subjected to research unless there is reason to believe that they might be beneficial. Null results, therefore, cry out for an explanation. What went wrong? The answer to that question has serious implications for the validity of the treatment concept, the operation of programs that provide the treatment, and any subsequent research done on the treatment. It is most important to interpret the nature of the failure (Suchman, 1967; Weiss, 1972). The first hypothesis that should be considered is that the research failed, not the treatment. Given the difficulty of conducting treatment effectiveness research, it is not implausible that (1) a given research study was statistically underpowered, (2) outcome variables were misspecified or inappropriately or insensitively measured, (3) treatment was confounded with an exogenous suppressor variable, (4) inappropriate statistical adjustments were used to equate nonrandomized groups, or (5) the study fell into any of a host of other pitfalls inherent to treatment effectiveness research. However, null results should not be accepted unless the research circumstances are sufficient to make them credible (for more extensive discussion of this matter, see Sechrest, 1986b; Yeaton, 1986).

If it appears that the null result probably did not arise from methodological failings, attention should turn to the implementation or delivery of the treatment. At issue here is whether the intended treatment was delivered or, if not, whether sufficient treatment was delivered to produce an effect. In practical treatment situations, it is not uncommon for high proportions of the target population to fail to receive treatment, drop out of treatment shortly after it commences, or receive weak, inconsistent, or diluted treatment. The evidence that bears on this issue is found in data that describe the nature and extent of the treatment received by each experimental subject. The role of treatment theory in this instance is to provide a framework that permits judgment about how treatment should be quantified, what constitute appropriate dimensions of strength and integrity, which treatment components or combinations are essential, and so forth.

Only when adequate methodology and adequate treatment implementation are established can null results be interpreted as indicative of failure of the treatment concept or theory. Even then, however, it is not necessarily appropriate to abandon the treatment concept. For complex treatments, some diagnosis of the treatment failure is required. Which step in the expected causal process failed to occur and why? Can it be easily remedied, or was it a fundamental failure? Does the nature of this failure suggest an alternate treatment theory that might be more effective? The answers to such questions are important for movement beyond a treatment failure toward development of better treatment concepts. Treatment theory serves to guide the collection of data that reflect important details of the causal process, and it also serves as the framework within which treatment failure is probed and interpreted. In the case of treatment effectiveness research that results in a finding of beneficial treatment effects, two related matters are of particular interest.

First, for practical purposes, it is important to understand just what, in fact, produced the result. A researcher must be sure that the "active ingredient" in the treatment (those components of the treatment bundle that were responsible for the effect) has been identified. Without that knowledge, an investigator or practitioner can only mechanically reapply the same bundle, hoping for the same effect in each application. Here, the role of treatment theory and its supporting evidence is obvious. Second, limits on generalizability of the effect must be established. As Campbell (1986) has argued, this is primarily a matter of determining which other situations are similar to the research situation in crucial ways. This kind of analysis requires the researcher to know on which parameters of the research situation the results are contingent. If, for example, the researcher knows that the treatment interacts with subject characteristics of a certain sort, a judgment can be made about whether it will be successful among various target populations that differ on those characteristics. If it is known that the treatment is relatively unaffected by variations in the delivery system, there can be greater confidence that implementation at another site will yield comparable results. As noted earlier, good treatment theory identifies the dimensions on which important variability might occur and permits their inclusion in the research.

Implications of a Theory Orientation for
Treatment Research

To guide and integrate method with theory in treatment effectiveness research and thus to gain the benefits described in this chapter, a type of research is required that is different in many ways from what is now conventional. There is the obvious necessity of developing treatment theory to describe what goes on inside the black box between treatment inputs and outputs. Theory must come from somewhere, however, and the most appropriate source is prior research and familiarity with the phenomena involved in a given treatment situation. Thus, theory-guided treatment research must be programmatic and cumulative in the conceptual sense; present practices are more aptly characterized as cumulations of studies conducted in relative independence from one another.

Perhaps more striking is the highly differentiated and multivariate research plan that must accompany this style of research. The simple one-shot, independent-variable/dependent-variable experiment that coincides well with the generic black box depiction of cause-and-effect relations is empirically meager as well as conceptually thin by the standards of theory-oriented treatment research. Instead, such research must be characterized by a host of preliminary studies and side studies and by a highly differentiated measurement scheme going well beyond an independent variable and a few dependent variables. Preliminary studies may be necessary to develop a basis for theory, address issues of dosage or treatment strength, identify appropriate covariates, explore the properties of various candidate measures, and so forth. Side studies may be necessary to address rival hypotheses, unbundle treatment components, examine selection or attrition events, and the like. A highly differentiated measurement scheme is necessary to give the researcher sufficient data on the details of the methods, the treatment implementation, the treatment process, and the expected and unexpected outcomes, so that all of the essential details can be represented and the final results of the study can be properly understood and interpreted.

Obviously, not all treatment effectiveness research must be conducted in this mode. There is a case to be made for testing promising treatments as molar wholes (in other words, black boxes) and exploring the details only after determining that they do have beneficial effects (Campbell, 1986). This reasoning applies more persuasively to simple treatments, since with complex treatments the task of designing research capable of detecting effects and determining the reasons for failure requires relatively detailed advance hypothesizing about the treatment process. More likely, research will lie somewhere between the extremes of the highly differentiated theory-oriented style and the crude, overly simplistic black box style. Even a small step, such as hypothesizing a few intervening variables or mediating processes to come between treatment input and output, and measuring and testing for their role, would greatly improve the research on many complex treatments.

Concluding Recommendations

It is fitting to conclude this chapter with a set of recommendations for the development of treatment theory:

1. Define the problem exactly, specifying its etiology if possible, its magnitude, why it is not self-limiting, where or in what persons or groups it occurs, and its consequences.
2. Define the treatment in terms of what are presumed to be the specific effective ingredients. Formulate a concept of strength of treatment and specify the range within which the planned treatment is likely to lie and the minimal regimen or operationalization necessary to deliver that treatment at effective strength.
3. Describe the mechanisms by which the planned treatment is supposed to have its effects. Specify any variables that are expected to mediate the effects of the treatment and the sequence of steps expected to occur between initial application of the treatment and the occurrence of its effects.
4. Define the desired outcomes as precisely as possible. Specify the minimal magnitudes of effects thought to be interesting, the maximal magnitude thought to be likely, and the timing with which such effects are expected to occur.

Finally, I offer a guided fantasy: Imagine a research community in which every report of a treatment effectiveness study includes a section labeled "treatment theory," which is considered as obligatory as the customary introduction, methods, results, and discussion sections. This chapter is intended to suggest just how much difference it might make to the validity of treatment research if this fantasy became reality.

References

Adelman, M. S. "Intervention Theory and Evaluating Efficacy." *Evaluation Review*, 1986, *10*, 65–83.

Ashby, W. R. *Introduction to Cybernetics.* London: Chapman & Hall, 1956.

Baker, F., and Intagliata, J. "Quality of Life in the Evaluation of Community Support Systems." *Evaluation and Program Planning*, 1982, *5*, 69–79.

Bickman, L. "Improving Established Statewide Programs: A Component Theory of Evaluation." *Evaluation Review*, 1985, *9*, 189–208.

Bickman, L. "The Functions of Program Theory." In L. Bickman (ed.), *Using Program Theory in Evaluation.* New Directions for Program Evaluation, no. 33. San Francisco: Jossey-Bass, 1987.

Boruch, R. F., and Gomez, M. "Sensitivity, Bias, and Theory in Impact Evaluations." *Professional Psychology,* 1977, *8,* 411–434.

Bougon, M. G. "Uncovering Cognitive Maps: The Self-Q Technique." In G. Morgan (ed.), *Beyond Method: A Study of Organization of Research Strategies.* Newbury Park, Calif.: Sage, 1983.

Brinberg, D., and McGrath, J. E. *Validity and the Research Process.* Newbury Park, Calif.: Sage, 1985.

Brownell, K. D., Marlatt, G. A., Lichtenstein, E., and Wilson, G. T. "Understanding and Preventing Relapse." *American Psychologist,* 1986, *41,* 765–782.

Campbell, D. T. "Relabeling Internal and External Validity for Applied Social Scientists." In W.M.K. Trochim (ed.), *Advances in Quasi-Experimental Design and Analysis.* New Directions for Program Evaluation, no. 31. San Francisco: Jossey-Bass, 1986.

Campbell, D. T., and Stanley, J. C. *Experimental and Quasi-Experimental Designs for Research.* Skokie, Ill.: Rand McNally, 1966.

Caplan, N. "Treatment Intervention and Reciprocal Interaction Effects." *Journal of Social Issues,* 1968, *24,* 63–88.

Carver, R. P. "Two Dimensions of Tests: Psychometric and Edumetric." *American Psychologist,* 1974, *29,* 512–518.

Chamberlin, T. C. "The Method of Multiple Working Hypotheses." *Science,* 1965, *148* (3671), 754–759.

Chandler, M. J. "Egocentrism and Antisocial Behavior: The Assessment and Training of Social Perspective-Taking Skills." *Developmental Psychology,* 1973, *9,* 326–333.

Chen, H. T., and Rossi, P. H. "The Multi-Goal, Theory-Driven Approach to Evaluation: A Model Linking Basic and Applied Social Science." *Social Forces,* 1980, *59,* 106–122.

Chen, H. T., and Rossi, P. H. "Evaluating with Sense: The Theory-Driven Approach." *Evaluation Review,* 1983, *7,* 283–302.

Cohen, P. "To Be or Not to Be: Control and Balancing of Type I and Type II Errors." *Evaluation and Program Planning,* 1982, *5,* 247–253.

Conrad, K. J., and Miller, T. Q. "Measuring and Testing Program Philosophy: A Framework for Implementation and Evaluation." In L. Bickman (ed.), *Using Program Theory in Evaluation.* New Directions for Program Evaluation, no. 33. San Francisco: Jossey-Bass, 1987.

Cook, T. D., and Campbell, D. T. (eds.). *Quasi-Experimentation: Design and Analysis Issues for Field Settings.* Boston: Houghton Mifflin, 1979.

Cook, T. J., and Poole, W. K. "Treatment Implementation and Statistical Power: A Research Note." *Evaluation Review,* 1982, *6,* 425–430.

Cordray, D. S. "Quasi-Experimental Analysis: A Mixture of Methods and Judgment." In W.M.K. Trochim (ed.), *Advances in Quasi-Experimental Design and Analysis.* New Directions for Program Evaluation, no. 31. San Francisco: Jossey-Bass, 1986.

Cordray, D. S., and Lipsey, M. W. "Evaluation 1986: Program Evaluation and Program Research." In D. S. Cordray and M. W. Lipsey (eds.), *Evaluation Studies Review Annual.* Vol. 11. Newbury Park, Calif.: Sage, 1987.

Crano, W. D., and Messe, L. A. "Assessing and Redressing Comprehension Artifacts in Social Intervention Research." *Evaluation Review,* 1985, *9,* 144–172.

Datta, L. "Does It Work When It Has Been Tried? And Half Full or Half Empty?" *Journal of Career Education,* 1976, *2,* 38–55.

Datta, L. "Interpreting Data: A Case Study from the Career Intern Program Evaluation." *Evaluation Review,* 1980, *4,* 481–506.

Dunford, F. W., and Elliott, D. S. "Identifying Career Offenders Using Self-Reported Data." *Journal of Research in Crime and Delinquency,* 1984, *21,* 57–86.

Einhorn, H. I., and Hogarth, R. M. "Judging Probable Cause." *Psychological Bulletin*, 1986, *99*, 3–19.

Elliott, D. S., Dunford, F. W., and Huizinga, D. "The Identification and Prediction of Career Offenders Utilizing Self-Reported and Official Data." In J. D. Burchard and S. N. Burchard (eds.), *The Prevention of Delinquent Behavior*. Newbury Park, Calif.: Sage, 1986.

Finney, J. W., and Moos, R. H. "Environmental Assessment and Evaluation Research: Examples from Mental Health and Substance Abuse Programs." *Evaluation and Program Planning*, 1984, *7*, 151–167.

Glaser, B. G., and Strauss, A. L. *The Discovery of Grounded Theory: Strategies of Qualitative Research*. Hawthorne, N.Y.: Aldine, 1967.

Gottfredson, G. D. "A Theory-Ridden Approach to Program Evaluation: A Method for Stimulating Researcher-Implementer Collaboration." *American Psychologist*, 1984, *39*, 1101–1112.

Hawkins, D. F. "Applied Research and Social Theory." *Evaluation Quarterly*, 1978, *2*, 141–152.

Holland, P. W. "Statistics and Causal Inference." *Journal of the American Statistical Association*, 1986, *81*, 945–960.

Howard, K. L., Kopta, S. M., Krause, M. S., and Orlinsky, D. E. "The Dose-Effect Relationship in Psychotherapy." *American Psychologist*, 1986, *41*, 159–164.

Johnston, I., Ettema, I., and Davidson, T. *An Evaluation of Freestyle: A Television Series to Reduce Sex-Role Stereotypes*. Ann Arbor: Institute for Social Research, University of Michigan, 1980.

Judd, C. M., and Kenny, D. A. "Process Analysis: Estimating Mediation in Treatment Evaluations." *Evaluation Review*, 1981, *5*, 602–619.

Kleinman, A. "Some Uses and Misuses of the Social Sciences in Medicine." In D. W. Fiske and R. A. Schweder (eds.), *Meta-Theory in Social Science: Pluralisms and Subjectivities*. Chicago: University of Chicago Press, 1986.

Kutchinsky, B. "The Effect of Easy Availability of Pornography on the Incidence of Sex Crimes: The Danish Experience." *Journal of Social Issues*, 1973, *29*, 163–181.

Lipsey, M. W. "A Scheme for Assessing Measurement Sensitivity in Program Evaluation and Other Applied Research." *Psychological Bulletin*, 1983, *94*, 152–165.

Lipsey, M. W. *Design Sensitivity: Statistical Power for Experimental Research*. Newbury Park, Calif.: Sage, 1990.

Lipsey, M. W., and Pollard, J. A. "Driving Toward Theory in Program Evaluation: More Models to Choose from." *Evaluation and Program Planning*, 1989, *12*, 317–328.

Lipsey, M. W., and others. "Evaluation: The State of the Art and the Sorry State of the Science." In D. S. Cordray (ed.), *Utilizing Prior Research in Evaluation Planning*. New Directions for Program Evaluation, no. 27. San Francisco: Jossey-Bass, 1985.

Loeber, R., and Stouthamer-Loeber, M. "The Prediction of Delinquency." In H. C. Quay (ed.), *Handbook of Juvenile Delinquency*. New York: Wiley, 1987.

McClintock, C. "Conceptual and Action Heuristics: Program Theory Tools for the Formative Evaluator." In L. Bickman (ed.), *Using Program Theory in Evaluation*. New Directions for Program Evaluation, no. 33. San Francisco: Jossey-Bass, 1987.

Mark, M. M. "Treatment Implementation, Statistical Power, and Internal Validity." *Evaluation Review*, 1983, *7*, 543–549.

Mark, M. M. "What Have We Learned About Studying Causal Process?" Paper presented at the annual meeting of the American Evaluation Association, Kansas City, Missouri, Oct. 1986.

Miller, W. R. "Motivation for Treatment: A Review with Special Emphasis on Alcoholism." *Psychological Bulletin*, 1985, *98*, 84–107.

O'Sullivan, E., Burleson, G. W., and Lamb, W. E. "Avoiding Evaluation Cooptation: Lessons from a Renal Dialysis Evaluation." *Evaluation and Program Planning*, 1985, *8*, 255–259.

Patterson, G. R. "Performance Models for Antisocial Boys." *American Psychologist*, 1986, *41*, 432–444.

Platt, J. R. "Strong Inference." *Science*, 1964, *146* (3642), 347–353.

Reichardt, C. S. "The Statistical Analysis of Data from Non-Equivalent Group Designs." In T. D. Cook and D. T. Campbell (eds.), *Quasi-Experimentation: Design and Analysis Issues for Field Settings*. Skokie, Ill.: Rand McNally, 1979.

Reichardt, C. S. "On the Logic and Practice of Assessing Cause." Paper presented at the annual meeting of the American Educational Research Association, Montreal, Apr. 1983.

Reichardt, C. S., and Gollob, H. F. "Satisfying the Constraints of Causal Modeling." In W.M.K. Trochim (ed.), *Advances in Quasi-Experimental Design and Analysis*. New Directions for Program Evaluation, no. 31. San Francisco: Jossey-Bass, 1986.

Rezmovic, E. L. "Assessing Treatment Implementation amid the Slings and Arrows of Reality." *Evaluation Review*, 1984, *8*, 187–204.

Rindskopf, D. "New Developments in Selection Modeling for Quasi-Experimentation." In W.M.K. Trochim (ed.), *Advances in Quasi-Experimental Design and Analysis*. New Directions for Program Evaluation, no. 31. San Francisco: Jossey-Bass, 1986.

Rosen, A., and Proctor, E. K. "Specifying the Treatment Process: The Basis for Effectiveness Research." *Journal of Social Service Research*, 1978, *2*, 25–43.

Rossi, P. H. "Issues in the Evaluation of Human Services Delivery." *Evaluation Quarterly*, 1978, *2*, 573–599.

Rossi, P. H., Berk, R. A., and Lenihan, K. J. *Money, Work, and Crime: Experimental Evidence*. San Diego: Academic Press, 1980.

Rossi, P. H., and Wright, J. D. "Evaluation Research: An Assessment." *Annual Review of Sociology*, 1984, *10*, 331–352.

Rubin, D. B. "Estimating Causal Effects of Treatments in Randomized and Nonrandomized Studies." *Journal of Educational Psychology*, 1974, *66*, 688–701.

Runyan, W. M. "A Stage-State Analysis of the Life Course." *Journal of Personality and Social Psychology*, 1980, *38*, 951–962.

St. Pierre, R. G., and Proper, E. C. "Attrition: Identification and Exploration in the National Follow-Through Evaluation." *Evaluation Review*, 1978, *2*, 153–166.

Scheirer, M. A. "Program Theory and Implementation Theory: Implications for Evaluators." In L. Bickman (ed.), *Using Program Theory in Evaluation*. New Directions for Program Evaluation, no. 33. San Francisco: Jossey-Bass, 1987.

Scheirer, M. A., and Rezmovic, E. L. "Measuring the Degree of Program Implementation: A Methodological Review." *Evaluation Review*, 1983, *7*, 599–633.

Schneider, A. L., and Darcy, R. E. "Policy Implications of Using Significance Tests in Evaluation Research." *Evaluation Review*, 1984, *8*, 573–580.

Scriven, M. "Maximizing the Power of Causal Investigations: The Modus Operandi Method." In W. J. Popham (ed.), *Evaluation in Education: Current Applications*. Berkeley, Calif.: McCutchan, 1974.

Sechrest, L. B. "Modes and Methods of Personality Research." *Journal of Personality*, 1986a, *54*, 318–331.

Sechrest, L. B. "What Have We Learned About Interpreting No-Difference Findings?" Paper presented at the annual meeting of the American Evaluation Association, Kansas City, Missouri, 1986b.

Sechrest, L. B., and Yeaton, W. H. "Empirical Bases for Estimating Effect Size." In R. F. Boruch, P. M. Wortman, and D. S. Cordray (eds.), *Reanalyzing Program Evaluations*. San Francisco: Jossey-Bass, 1981.

Sechrest, L. B., and Yeaton, W. H. "Magnitudes of Experimental Effects in Social Science Research." *Evaluation Review*, 1982, *6*, 579–600.

Sechrest, L. B., and others. "Some Neglected Problems in Evaluation Research: Strength and Integrity of Treatments." In L. B. Sechrest and others (eds.), *Evaluation Studies Review Annual*. Vol. 4. Newbury Park, Calif.: Sage, 1979.

Shapiro, J. Z. "The Social Costs of Methodological Rigor: A Note on the Problem of Massive Attrition." *Evaluation Review*, 1984a, *8*, 705–712.

Shapiro, J. Z. "Social Justice and Educational Evaluation: Normative Implications of Alternative Criteria for Program Assessment." *Educational Theory*, 1984b, *34*, 137–149.

Sherrill, S. "Toward a Coherent View of Evaluation." *Evaluation Review*, 1984, *8*, 443–466.

Smith, A., Cardillo, J. E., and Choate, R. O. "Age-Based Transition Periods and the Outcome of Mental Health Treatment." *Evaluation and Program Planning*, 1984, *7*, 237–244.

Snowden, L. R. "Treatment Participation and Outcome in a Program for Problem Drinker-Drivers." *Evaluation and Program Planning*, 1984, *7*, 65–71.

Suchman, E. A. *Evaluation Research: Principles and Practices in Public Service and Social Programs*. New York: Russell Sage Foundation, 1967.

Taber, M. A., and Poertner, J. P. "Modeling Service Delivery as a System of Transitions." *Evaluation Review*, 1981, *5*, 549–566.

Trochim, W.M.K. "Framing the Evaluation Question: Some Useful Strategies." Paper presented at the joint meeting of the Evaluation Research Society and Evaluation Network, Chicago, Oct. 1983.

Trochim, W.M.K. "Pattern Matching, Validity, and Conceptualization in Program Evaluation." *Evaluation Review*, 1985, *9*, 575–604.

Trochim, W.M.K. (ed.). *Advances in Quasi-Experimental Design and Analysis*. New Directions for Program Evaluation, no. 31. San Francisco: Jossey-Bass, 1986a.

Trochim, W.M.K. "Editor's Notes." In W.M.K. Trochim (ed.), *Advances in Quasi-Experimental Design and Analysis*. New Directions for Program Evaluation, no. 31. San Francisco: Jossey-Bass, 1986b.

Wang, M. C., and Walberg, H. J. "Evaluating Educational Programs: An Integrative, Causal-Modeling Approach." *Educational Evaluation and Policy Analysis*, 1983, *5*, 347–366.

Weinholtz, D., and Friedman, C. P. "Conducting Qualitative Studies Using Theory and Previous Research." *Evaluation and the Health Professions*, 1985, *8*, 149–176.

Weiss, C. H. *Evaluation Research: Methods of Assessing Program Effectiveness*. Englewood Cliffs, N.J.: Prentice Hall, 1972.

Wholey, J. S. "Evaluability Assessment: Developing Program Theory." In L. Bickman (ed.), *Using Program Theory in Evaluation*. New Directions for Program Evaluation, no. 33. San Francisco: Jossey-Bass, 1987.

Wilkins, W. "Placebo Problems in Psychotherapy Research: Social-Psychological Alternatives to Chemotherapy Concepts." *American Psychologist*, 1986, *41*, 551–556.

Yeaton, W. H. "Proceed With Caution: Using No-Difference Findings to Eliminate Validity Threats." Paper presented at the annual meeting of the American Evaluation Association, Kansas City, Missouri, Oct. 1986.

Yeaton, W. H., and Sechrest, L. B. "Critical Dimensions in the Choice and Maintenance of Successful Treatments: Strength, Integrity, and Effectiveness." *Journal of Consulting and Clinical Psychology*, 1981, *49*, 156–167.

Yeaton, W. H., Wortman, P. M., and Langberg, N. "Differential Attrition: Estimating the Effect of Crossovers on the Evaluation of a Medical Technology." *Evaluation Review*, 1983, *7*, 831–840.

MARK W. LIPSEY is professor in the Department of Human Services, Vanderbilt University, Nashville, Tennessee.

This chapter discusses the generalization of causal relationships and offers an applied, meta-analytical approach.

A Quasi-Sampling Theory of the Generalization of Causal Relationships

Thomas D. Cook

The Language of Causal Generalization

Campbell (1957) and Cronbach (1982) have each claimed that causal generalization is concerned with drawing conclusions about four entities. The first is *treatments,* the causal agents whose effects are to be assessed. Rarely do we want to make inferences about the specific details of a particular manipulation. Instead, we want the manipulation to represent a class designated in abstract (that is, general) language. Thus, we refer to "external threat" as a cause of in-group cohesion and make no attempt to provide an exhaustive description of what experiments do to induce such threat. Similarly, we refer to Head Start as a cause of academic achievement in preschoolers without providing a list of the specific Head Start centers in a sample.

Second, we also seek to draw conclusions about *observations,* especially those that represent potential treatment effects. In a study of external threat as a cause of in-group cohesion, we would have little conceptual

A version of this paper was published in L. Sechrest, E. Perrin, and J. Bunker (eds.), *Research Methodology: Strengthening Causal Interpretations of Nonexperimental Data* (Conference proceedings), Washington, D.C.: Agency for Health Care Policy and Research, Public Health Service, U.S. Department of Health and Human Services, May 1990. Helpful feedback was provided by Melvyn M. Mark and William R. Shadish, Jr., and their assistance, both now and in the past, is gratefully acknowledged.

interest in the specifics of how in-group cohesion was measured. The inference that we target is about in-group cohesion per se. Similarly, we have little interest in the particular achievement test used to assess Head Start achievement gains. We want to generalize to achievement writ large.

Once we are confident of the general, theoretical labels to attach to a cause and effect—what Cook and Campbell (1979) call "construct validity"—we still need to know in which *populations* and *settings* the cause and effect are related. Such populations and settings constitute the third and fourth entities to which generalization is often sought, and they correspond with Cook and Campbell's explication of external validity. (Campbell [1957] has added a fifth entity to the list—*time*—for researchers may want to generalize to a particular historical period, such as the 1970s, or conclude that a causal relationship is universal and thus holds for all times.) Causal generalization is a matter of specifying the range of application of a causal relationship that has been demonstrated with at least one instance of a treatment and outcome and at least one sample of persons and settings.

We make a distinction between causal connections and causal explanations (Collingwood, 1940; Cook and Campbell, 1979, 1986; Gasking, 1957; Mackie, 1974). Causal connections are implicit in such statements as "External threat causes in-group cohesion," "Head Start increases achievement," "Aspirin reduces headaches," and "School desegregation causes white flight." These examples are characterized by a manipulable treatment specified in general language, a response specified in the same type of language, and a causal connection that describes the nature of the link between the two; if one is made to vary, the other varies with it and would not have varied had the cause not been present.

Such descriptive causal connections are to be distinguished from causal explanations that identify *how* or *why* a causal connection occurs. Why does external threat cause in-group cohesion? Why does Head Start raise achievement? Why does aspirin reduce headaches? Why do whites flee when schools desegregate? Causal explanation involves specifying the full set of conditions promoting the cause-effect connection, which often entails identifying the mediational forces set in motion when the treatment varies and without which the effect would not occur. This chapter is about the generalization of descriptive causal connections, though we shall see that causal explanation is often advocated as a means of promoting such generalization.

Cronbach (1982) has claimed that there are two ways of framing the causal generalization question. I explicate his analysis below. To make the discussion clear, I often refer to the literature on patient education and its causal influence in promoting recovery from surgery (Devine, 1992; Devine and Cook, 1983; Devine and others, 1988; O'Connor and others, 1989).

Cronbach's First Problem of Causal Generalization

Cronbach's (1982) first problem involves the use of sample data to generalize to target cause-and-effect constructs and to target populations of persons and settings. For example, one might ask whether patient education (the target cause) promotes physical recovery (the target effect) among surgical patients (the target population of persons) in American hospitals (the target universe of settings). In order to answer this question, researchers must choose manipulations and measures and sample patients and hospitals so as to "represent" these target entities.

However, empirical results often force researchers to specify boundary conditions that limit the generalizability of the causal connection under study. Thus, the planned causal agent—patient education—might need to be respecified as *pre*surgical or *post*surgical patient education because only one of them is causally related to recovery from surgery. Similarly, a causal connection might be supported for cholecystectomy patients (persons needing gallbladder surgery) but not for patients with other diagnoses. Data can sometimes lead researchers to think in terms of constructs and categories that are more general than those with which they began a research program. Thus, the creative analyst of patient education studies might surmise that the treatment is a subclass of interventions increasing "perceived control" or that recovery from surgery can be treated as a subclass of "personal coping." But whatever the level of generality involved, the conceptual issue is always the same: How do we generalize from a sample of instances and the data patterns associated with them to particular entities, populations, universes, categories, or classes (terms that we use interchangeably)?

The ability to generalize with confidence is important to many constituency groups. On the one hand, practitioners such as hospital administrators want the studies that they commission to apply to the unique settings and populations for which they are responsible. They have little interest in other settings or groups or in a treatment's theoretical integrity, that is, its correspondence with a protocol derived from a theorist's analysis. They value only those treatment forms that are viable in their hospitals. On the other hand, all theorists want to generalize to the specific cause-and-effect constructs on which their theories are built. Otherwise, relevance is diminished. But some universe-bound theorists want to generalize to particular populations (such as types of hospitals or types of people) because their theories are about these types in particular. The ability to generalize more widely is not as important to them as it is to those more universalist scholars who measure the success of their theories by the breadth of their application across settings, persons, times, and constructs. Their wish is for causal statements requiring no qualifications about the

conditions within which the statement is true. (The epistemological so-
phistication of such universalist theorists is another matter; see Mackie,
1974.)

The task of framing causal generalization in terms of the correspondence between samples (or cases, instances, exemplars, and so on) and the
populations, universes, constructs, categories, or classes that they represent invites the suggestion that causal generalization is best promoted
through the well-known sampling procedures that statisticians have invented to justify inferences from samples to populations. These procedures
have been dramatically successful across a wide range of practical applications, especially in survey research and quality control in industry. The
crucial element in sampling theory involves selection of units with known
probability from some clearly designated universe so as to match the
sample and population distributions on all (measured and unmeasured)
attributes within known limits of sampling error. Some statisticians write
as though confident causal generalization depends exclusively on random
sampling. Thus, as Lavori, Louis, Bailar, and Polansky (1986, pp. 62–63)
opine,

> So far we have dealt with methods for ensuring that the analysis of a
> parallel-treatment study correctly assesses the relative effects of treat-
> ment on patients enrolled in that study. The investigator must also
> consider whether the results can properly be extended to patients out-
> side the study; we refer to this issue as generalizability. . . . Unless there
> is random sampling from a well-defined population (not to be confused
> with random allocation of treatment), the question of generalizability
> may not be completely resolvable. Nevertheless a brief discussion of
> selection criteria and a concise description of the clinically relevant facts
> about the patients chosen for study can go a long way toward meeting
> this objective.

Note this last disclaimer, which I elaborate on later, for it suggests that
researchers need not throw in the towel if random selection is not possible.
Note also that these four statisticians mention only one domain across
which causal connections are to be generalized: populations of persons.
We need to also ask about the relevance of the formal sampling ideal for
generalizing to causes, effects, settings, and times.

In a book on statistical methods for causal generalization, Kish (1987)
advocates the statistician's traditional two-step ideal: the random selection
of units for enhancing generalization and the random assignment of units
to different treatments for promoting causal inference. But Kish frankly
acknowledges that this ideal is rarely feasible, and he explicitly chooses not
to deal with how manipulations and measures might be selected so as to
represent cause-and-effect constructs, even though such constructs are

indispensable to causal generalization. Kish suggests that the statistical theory that he prefers cannot constitute a *comprehensive* practical framework for causal generalization, though it may sometimes promote generalization to populations of persons and settings. Later, I examine how well classical sampling theory promotes inferences about Cronbach's first type of causal generalization.

Cronbach's Second Problem of Causal Generalization

Cronbach's second problem of causal generalization involves generalization from samples and whichever universes they represent to populations that are manifestly different from those sampled. This entails the *transfer* of causal knowledge to novel cause-and-effect constructs, to novel classes of persons and settings, and to future time periods.

The utility of such causal transfer is indisputable. Most theorists value causal propositions that are so universal they hold for all persons in all settings at all times and with all imaginable ways of conceptualizing a class of causes or effects (Calder, Phillips, and Tybout, 1981, 1982; Kruglanski and Kroy, 1975). Such theorists assign less value to causal propositions that are hedged with so many boundary conditions that their predictive generality is minimal (Bandura, 1986).

Causal knowledge that is broadly transferable is also valuable for more applied purposes. At the local level, potential users of information will be more confident that a causal connection demonstrated elsewhere will also hold in the settings for which they are responsible, even though the connection may never have been explicitly tested there (Cronbach and others, 1980). At a more central level in the policy process, decision makers will feel more confident that the changes they legislate will be broadly implementable and generally effective across an entire nation or state, even though there is considerable local variability in how a policy is administered (Cook, Leviton, and Shadish, 1985).

Causal explanation is widely invoked as the means for transferring knowledge to never-studied contexts (see Cronbach and others, 1980). The assumption behind this belief is that an understanding of how or why a phenomenon comes about permits recreation of that phenomenon *wherever* and *however* its essential causal ingredients can be brought together. For instance, knowledge of how electricity is generated allows us to provide such power to satellites in space, where electricity may never have been available or studied before; knowledge of the pharmacologically active ingredients of aspirin might allow inventive persons to create the drug's equivalent out of local plants that have never before been used to cure headaches. The presumption is that knowledge of the complete causal system (as with electricity) or of the total set of causally efficacious components (as with aspirin) makes it easier to reproduce a given causal connection in a wide variety of forms and settings, including those previously unexamined (Bhaskar, 1975). This is why causal explanation is often considered the Holy Grail of science.

But such complete knowledge is rarely available in the social sciences. Explanatory questions such as "Why does patient education promote recovery?" presuppose valid answers to their descriptive causal counterpart questions. They also assume that well-corroborated substantive theories are available whose constructs are well specified and can be validly measured. And, finally, each supposes that other models, with or without the same constructs, cannot be fit to the data equally well or better. This last assumption is rarely valid (Glymour, 1987). It should come as no surprise, therefore, that we do not yet know why patient education is effective, despite about 150 studies on the topic and the availability of numerous explanatory theories that emphasize constructs from quite different classes, including the physiological, psychological, and social (Devine, 1992). Nor do we know why whites flee schools as blacks enter them, though here the descriptive causal connection is more elusive than is the case with patient education. Complete explanatory causal knowledge is useful for the knowledge transfer that Cronbach and others value. The key question concerns how often useful explanatory causal knowledge can be gained given that *complete* causal knowledge is not a reality.

Within the framework of these issues of causal generalization, this chapter has a number of goals. The first is to examine the roles that random selection can realistically play in generalizing to all four of the target entities in Cronbach's first framing of the causal generalization issue. The second is to examine Cronbach's second framing of the issue in order to assess the roles that causal explanation can realistically play in justifying inferences from samples or instances to populations or classes that have manifestly different characteristics. The third is to explicate an alternative comprehensive theory of causal generalization that is based on five principles, none of which requires random sampling and all of which apply to both of Cronbach's types of causal generalization. This alternative theory is less elegant than sampling theory or complete causal explanation, but it is more widely feasible and likely to be more useful. Its origins lie in the theories of classification and category membership (see, for example, Lakoff, 1985; Smith and Medlin, 1981) that undergird modern attempts in psychometrics to use measures and manipulations to draw conclusions about general constructs. But I contend that generalizations about human populations and physical or social settings can be generated the same way. Finally, the fourth goal is to develop the argument that the alternative theory espoused is most applicable when multiple studies of a causal proposition are available. I exemplify this point by examining meta-analysis, a technique for quantitatively reviewing the literature, including that on causal connections (Glass, McGaw, and Smith, 1981; Hedges and

Olkin, 1985). I claim that meta-analysis probes both of Cronbach's types of causal generalization and that it is successful in this endeavor because it incorporates the five principles of causal generalization explicated.

These principles overlap with Mark's (1986) independent analysis of how similarity, heterogeneous irrelevancies, and explanation promote causal generalization. In his case and mine, there is a shared osmotic debt to Campbell's work on external validity and construct validity, especially as presented in Campbell (1969, 1978), Campbell and Fiske (1959), Campbell and Stanley (1966), Webb, Campbell, Schwartz, and Sechrest (1966), and Cook and Campbell (1979). No claim is made that all of Campbell's insights into the nonstatistical and nonexplanatory bases of causal generalization have been systematized here. My more modest goal is to increase awareness of the need for improved theories of causal generalization and to persuade theorists of method to consider nontraditional techniques for this purpose.

Causal Generalization Through Sampling Theory

Random Sampling and Inferences About Cause-and-Effect Constructs. Sampling theory requires a clearly designated population. It is relatively easy to develop such descriptions for many human populations and settings, such as cholecystectomy patients or American hospitals. However, the task is more difficult with the less material terms typically used to designate cause-and-effect constructs in the social and health sciences, for example, patient education, recovery from surgery, anxiety, or anomie. Scholars often disagree about what the components of a construct should be, what weight should be attached to any one of them, and how the components are related to each other.

Even if a comprehensive description were forthcoming, it would still be difficult to enumerate all of the instances of a cause or effect prior to random selection. Full enumeration is occasionally possible, as when a computer generates every two-digit addition or subtraction possibility to create the universe of all two-digit arithmetic problems. But this is an atypical case of interest to few. Most item enumeration involves subject matter experts explicating a construct, identifying components of a cause or an effect, and then crafting manipulations or measures that reflect these descriptions. Judgment is of the essence. There can be no presumption of generating the universe of all possible items or manipulations that measure a cause or an effect construct.

Still, judgment processes can result in long lists of possible manipulations or measures. Random selection rarely occurs from such lists, however. In experiments, implementation of even two planned variants of the same causal construct is rarely practical, though it is theoretically possible. In practice, additional resources are used to add new theory-based treatment or control groups, to increase the number of measurement waves, or to increase the number of units per cell of the design. It is difficult to justify a second planned treatment variant when one is already available, and, anyway, sampling theory requires many such variants if confident generalization is to result. This large sample requirement makes multiple variants of the same intervention unrealistic for most circumstances of interest.

It is easier to achieve multiple measures of an effect, however, especially when paper-and-pencil tests are used. Yet, it is noteworthy that causal research in field settings nearly always involves outcomes measures that are shorter than measures of the same constructs used in personality or aptitude testing. This is because field experimenters are always under pressure to measure many different outcome and moderator constructs and to restrict the total testing time. Measurement of just a few constructs with a high degree of validity is a lower priority, so cause-probing studies gravitate toward the assessment of many constructs, utilizing few items for any one of them. These practical considerations make random item selection—with its large sample requirement—rarely appropriate.

Theoretical examination of any social construct usually leads to the conclusion that it has many components, domains, or facets. Each of these requires multiple items if it is to be assessed well. The number of items per component can vary, of course, to reflect component differences in centrality. While item selection can take place at random to assess any one component, this is only practical when a research project involves a small number of constructs and components. This is a situation that researchers rarely face, so item selection tends to drift toward rational selection based on human judgments about the degree to which particular components are prototypical of a construct and the degree to which specific items are prototypical of the more important components. Early in his career, Cronbach called for random item selection (Cronbach, Rajaratram, and Gleser, 1967). But later he argued that item selection is less important than ensurance (Cronbach, Gleser, Nanda, and Rajaratram, 1972) and justification (Cronbach, 1985) that a construct description has captured all of the construct components of theoretical relevance.

Even so, calls are still heard for random rather than judgmental item sampling (for example, Wigdor and Green, 1986). But the frame from which items can be selected to represent a construct is less clear than the frame for selecting persons and settings to represent their respective populations. And resources are rarely available for generating the large number of items required to make large sample probabilistic techniques superior to judgmental selection, especially when many constructs have to be assessed or constructs are multidimensional (Lammlein, Peterson, and Rosse, 1987). I agree that, in theory, random selection is the superior way to sample causal manipulations and effect measures. But I argue that such selection can only be meaningfully implemented in the very rare context where field experiments are characterized by few constructs to be assessed, each construct has few components, many items are available for enumerating each component, the process for generating the item pool is unbiased, and resources are sufficient to permit selection of many items per component.

Random Selection and Populations of Persons and Settings. The use of random samples to generalize to specific populations of persons and settings is easier. However, practical constraints still limit the researcher's power to sample units at random. Not all of the individuals and organizations selected for a cause-probing study will agree to participate, and the units that agree are likely to be different in many ways from the units that refuse participation, leading to a mismatch between the targeted and achieved populations. A mismatch also arises when informed consent is a precondition for participation in a study. Generalization is then limited to the theoretically irrelevant circumstance where individuals are knowledgeable about a study and agree to be in it. Since most cause-probing research that takes place in field settings is also longitudinal, there will inevitably be some attrition as individuals die, move home, or are bored by the demands of treatment or measurement. Such posttreatment attrition has to be added to initial refusal rates when assessing the correspondence between the intended and achieved populations. High refusal and attrition rates do not render random selection meaningless, or even inferior to its alternatives, but they do attenuate its advantages.

No discussion of sampling realities in causal studies can be complete without mention of the financial costs of mounting an intervention at more than a handful of sites. Many interventions are expensive, and, by definition, their efficacy is not established. It does not make administrative sense, therefore, to fund a "representative" study with many randomly selected sites in order to test something that may not be effective. This administrative reality means that except for a small number of multimillion-dollar clinical trials in medicine and public health, few studies of ameliorative treatments have involved randomly chosen samples of persons and settings that were then randomly assigned to different treatments. And in these few cases, random selection was mostly from within some circumscribed entity, such as a small number of cities or hospitals in a particular city. It is rare to find experimental studies with units selected at random from a broad population. This rarity is no accident in light of the logistical and financial realities noted above.

A further "problem" with random selection has to do with the trade-offs that its implementation usually requires. Consider the trade-off between internal and external validity. Imagine drawing a random sample of respondents or sites and then randomly assigning them to different treatments. Treatment-correlated refusals would be anticipated whenever the treatments differ in intrinsic desirability, as they often do in field research. Such differential attrition creates the very group noncomparability that random assignment was designed to avoid. To prevent this, Riecken and Boruch (1974) have suggested that random assignment should be postponed until after respondents have (1) agreed to participate in the measurement framework for the entire course of a study, (2) been fully informed of the different treatments, and (3) agreed to participate in whichever treatment group the coin toss determines for them. This sampling strategy enhances internal validity because it reduces the rates of treatment-correlated refusal and attrition. However, external validity is compromised because more respondents are likely to refuse to be in the study when explicitly confronted with the measurement burdens and the possibility of being assigned to a less desirable treatment. This trade-off is not inevitable, but it is highly likely when measurement burdens are high, treatments differ in intrinsic desirability, and respondents learn about treatment differences.

The same trade-off also holds for quasi experiments. I recently helped design a study on the effects of a televised smoking cessation campaign in the Chicago Standard Metropolitan Statistical Area (Warnecke and others, 1991, 1992). Shows from the campaign were broadcast twice each evening on the network news for twenty-one days, with many different kinds of follow-up provided. There were two major options for sampling and treatment assignment. The population could be limited to smokers who reported watching the evening news regularly, say, five or more times per week. The treatment group would then consist of regular news watchers of the network broadcasting the antismoking materials, while the control group would be regular news watchers, at the same time, of a competing network. This plan maximizes internal validity under two assumptions: The two groups do not differ much, each being equally faithful in watching the network evening news; and the treatment contrast is large because faithful viewers of the target channel would watch more of the antismoking shows. But the choice of restricting the study to smokers who watch network news at least five times per week means that the results apply only to smokers who are also faithful viewers of a particular television channel. How these persons differ from other smokers is not clear, but it would not be easy to assume there are no differences.

The second sampling option also requires identification of smokers who prefer the news on one channel, but the viewing threshold is set lower, say, twice per week. The broader population sought now ensues, but so also do internal validity costs, for the size of the contrast between levels of viewing the antismoking materials is now reduced and there will almost certainly be some viewing by members of the control group. Given the primacy of internal validity, it is questionable whether random selection from meaningful populations can be as routinely used in cause-probing experimental studies as it is in, say, surveys designed to describe attributes of human populations.

Summary. Random sampling is of limited utility when causal generalization is at issue because the model is never relevant to making generalized inferences about manipulable causal agents, and it is rarely relevant to making generalized inferences about effects. As far as persons and settings are concerned, the model assumes sampling occurs from some meaningful population, though ethical, political, and logistical constraints often limit random selection to less meaningful populations. Moreover, there are many situations where random selection and its goals conflict with random assignment and its goals, though probing the generality of a causal connection clearly supposes the primacy of identifying a causal connection or assessing its generality; and realities of budget and control over treatment implementation quality and measurement validity often limit the selection of units to a small and geographically circumscribed population. It also must be remembered that random sampling is not relevant to generalization to future time periods or to Cronbach's second framing of the causal generalization issue, that is, generalization beyond target constructs and populations.

Taken together, these limitations indicate that random selection cannot be advocated as *the* model for causal generalization, despite the claims on its behalf by Lavori, Louis, Bailar, and Polansky (1986) and Kish (1987). Is there a viable alternative? This is the issue I now take up.

Causal Generalization and Five Principles of Construct Validation Applied to Cause-and-Effect Constructs

Samples of measures and manipulations are regularly used to draw conclusions about general cause-and-effect constructs, though the selection is rarely at random. Here, I identify the five principles that I think make this practice possible. I later ask whether they are also relevant for justifying inferences about persons and settings. I also explore how they are implicitly built into perhaps the most successful current method for causal generalization: meta-analysis.

Principle of Proximal Similarity. The precondition for construct validity is an exhaustive multivariate description of the target construct. This should be explicitly based on the prior literature, where available, and should also specify which of the construct's attributes are considered prototypical (Rosch, 1978). Operational instances are then selected to represent this theoretical description.

One criterion for selecting instances is their proximal similarity to the construct description (Campbell, 1969). That is, in the judgment of the focal research community, operational instances should embody most of the construct's identified components, especially those that are prototypical. The importance of prototypicality can be seen by conceptualizing construct validity in terms of pattern matching—postulating the multidimensional content of a construct and then selecting operational particulars that recreate this pattern of components. But matching cannot knowingly be achieved on all components and is most importantly achieved with those components that theoretical analysis suggests are central to the construct description. The similarity so achieved is proximal because the operations and constructs match in manifest characteristics and not necessarily in any of the more latent explanatory components that link a cause to an effect. A definition of proximal similarity framed in terms of causal mediational forces (Bhaskar, 1975) restricts construct validity to contexts where considerable explanation is already available. While such knowledge should be taken into account when it is available, proximal similarity refers to the correspondence in manifest descriptive attributes between a theoretical description and its operational representation(s).

Compared to random item selection, rational sampling for proximal similarity has several disadvantages. First, it achieves overlap between the construct and operations on a narrower range of variables; and, second, explicit theoretical justifications are needed for the components considered to be prototypical, and not everyone will agree on what these are. By itself, therefore, rational selection cannot make a totally persuasive case that a sample represents an identifiable target population. More is needed.

Principle of Heterogeneous Irrelevancies. Any single operational instance of a cause or an effect underrepresents the full set of relevant components and contains its own unique irrelevancies. Thus, attitude is measured using a paper-and-pencil measure that is irrelevant to the concept of attitude; Head Start is evaluated in some centers whose particular personnel constitute an irrelevancy; length of hospital stay is estimated from patient reports that may contain irrelevant memory biases. Knowledge of the omnipresence of such irrelevancies in cause-probing research has spurred the call for multiple over single operationalism (Webb, Campbell, Schwartz, and Sechrest, 1966). Multiple operationalism requires all of the operations used to index a construct to be proximally similar, but across the set of operations, the requirement is heterogeneity in all conceptual irrelevancies. The aspiration is to probe two things. The most important is whether the cause-effect relationship under investigation is obtained when a particular irrelevancy or set of irrelevancies is and is not present. This allows empirical assessment of the role of the irrelevancies and a direct test of the causal link when no irrelevancies, or the fewest number, are present. The fallback test is whether the causal relationship continues to hold when operational instances with and without the irrelevancy are combined. In combining across irrelevancies, we ask whether the irrelevancy makes a difference, about whether the causal relationship is obtained *despite* the irrelevancies.

Let me try to make the discussion more concrete. If we wanted to generalize to attitude and had data only from paper-and-pencil measures, then attitude and the mode of measurement would be hopelessly confounded. To disentangle them, direct observation and physiological measures might be added to create three modes of measurement, each being a theoretical irrelevancy but permitting us to probe whether the same causal sign is obtained with each method. When separate breakdowns cannot be made, the different operational instances have to be summed into a multimethod composite, which renders an explicitly falsificationist rationale less viable because we must blindly assume that any biases favoring one theoretically irrelevant interpretation are exactly counterbalanced by biases operating against this interpretation. Nonetheless, composite measures are still useful. They increase the degree of proximal similarity between operations and their referent constructs and help probe whether an effect is found when the total set of operational instances is imbued with many more irrelevant theories than a single measure or manipulation allows (Kuhn, 1962; Stegmuller, 1976). Multiple operations always reduce the threats to interpretation emanating from theoretically irrelevant sources of variance, especially when the data analysis can treat these irrelevancies as separate factors.

Brunswik (1955) is most closely associated with theoretical thinking about the heterogeneity of irrelevancies. He worked mostly in human perception, which he assumed is context-dependent. To illustrate this dependence, he used the homely example of studying facial characteristics. Staying with this example but translating it into the causal generalization context of interest here, we can imagine studying whether persons who squint are judged more sly than people who do not squint. Since squints exist only on faces, Brunswik maintained that they cannot and should not be abstracted from faces. Presumably, he would not favor studies in which respondents rate squints on otherwise masked faces. But decisions have to be made about which facial attributes to build into the research. Should there be details about eyes (their color or size), noses (their size or shape), facial contours (round or oval, and so on), chin forms (square, pointed, rounded), or other features? The size of pores, the length of eyelashes, and the number of wrinkles could also be incorporated into the stimulus materials. But in any one study we cannot vary—that is, make heterogeneous—all possible facial attributes. Hence fallible judgment based on theory or personal experience has to be used to decide on the attributes that are presumed to be more prototypical and hence deserving of deliberate variation in the research. There will doubtless be attributes whose potential relevance is indeterminate, perhaps as regards lip thickness or distance between the eyes. What is done with these depends largely on resources.

Brunswik does not advocate varying every contextual feature singly, as in a factorial experimental design. He prefers to sample combinations of facial attributes that meet two criteria: They co-occur with some regularity, and they are maximally different from each other. If a cause-effect relationship remains robust across all of the combinations of irrelevancies sampled, Brunswik would conclude that the relationship is independent of facial characteristics; and if the relationship occurred with certain kinds of faces, but not others, he would then claim to have specified some of the conditions under which a squint causes attributions of shiftiness.

Fisher (1935, p. 99) clearly noted the advantage of multiple irrelevancies when probing cause-effect relationships: "Any given conclusion . . . has a wider inductive base when inferred from an experiment in which the quantities of other ingredients have been varied, than it would have from any amount of experimentation, in which these had been kept strictly constant. . . . Standardization weakens rather than strengthens our ground for inferring a like result, when, as is invariably the case in practice, these conditions are somewhat varied." His insight is presumably based on the supposition that causal results that are demonstrably robust across many irrelevancies constitute multiple failed attempts to disconfirm the hypothesis of a *generalized* causal relationship. Are causal connections worth provisional treatment as general if researchers have deliberately incorporated into their research multiple sources of irrelevant heterogeneity, especially those that theory suggests are most likely to make a causal connection disappear?

Researchers with applied interests rarely want to examine robustness across all possible contexts, since there are usually specific human and physical contexts to which they want to generalize. Surgical patients and hospitals are not irrelevancies to scholars interested in patient education! But there are other irrelevancies for such scholars: the cities studied, the types of surgical patient, the ways in which recovery from surgery are measured. Applied researchers have a vested interest in any causal connection that is demonstrably robust across all the conceptual irrelevancies that operate within the surgery-hospital context that bounds their interests. Theorists, on the other hand, have an even broader conception of what is an "irrelevancy," with universalists aspiring to discover causal connections that hold for all settings, persons, times, and methods.

Given the importance just assigned to robust causal findings, I need to be more explicit than was Brunswik about the meaning of robustness. Many theorists believe that the world is more contingently ordered than universalist theorists would like to believe and that statistical main effects rarely describe the world accurately (Mackie, 1974). They contend that the world, including the social world, should be characterized more as a set of interconnected multivariate pretzels with causal feedback loops than as a series of causal arrows flying directly from A-the-cause to B-the-effect. Cronbach and Snow (1976) have examined many causal relationships in education and claim that complex statistical interactions are the norm, and

McGuire (1984) has claimed the same for social psychology. It is entirely possible, then, that if robustness were specified as *constancy of effect sizes,* few causal relationships in the social world would be robust.

However, robustness is better conceptualized as *constancy of causal direction.* That is, the sign linking the cause to the effect is constant across replications. Several factors argue in favor of this conceptualization. First, casual examination of many meta-analyses convinces us that causal signs tend to be similar across individual studies even when the effect sizes vary considerably. Second, the social policy world, it is difficult to shape legislation or regulations to suit local contingencies. Instead, the same plan has to be promulgated across an entire nation or state to avoid focused inequities among individual places or groups. Policymakers hope that a program or policy will have positive effects overall, despite variability in effect sizes from site to site and perhaps even a different causal sign for a minority of sites or groups. And, third, substantive theories should be built around causal relationships whose occurrence is particularly dependable as well as around theories whose consequences are obviously novel. This reduces the risk of theorizing about unstable phenomena, an unfortunate commonplace in much of today's social science! Since a definition of robustness in terms of effect sizes loses all of these advantages, I favor a looser criterion based on the stability of causal signs.

Principle of Discriminant Validity. Many of the irrelevancies that need to be ruled out in construct validation follow from the fact that measurement requires a data collection mode that is not itself part of the construct description. However, some irrelevancies are substantive and follow from the fact that nearly all theoretical constructs share some components. A decomposition of variance is therefore called for to probe whether a causal connection is truly from A to B or, instead, might be from some subset of A's components shared with C or D or might involve only a subset of B's components that are shared with E or F. The question then arises, Is an obtained causal relationship from A to B as hoped, or is it instead from A to E or F or, alternatively, from C or D to B?

Campbell and Fiske (1959) propose that an analysis testing cross-method generalizability should be complemented by an analysis capable of discriminating a target construct from its cognates. An example of their multitrait, multimethod approach to construct validation clarifies this point. When physicians or nurses in patient education studies know who is receiving an intervention, it is crucial to distinguish effects of the education from effects of the professionals' expectations for recovery. In order to make this distinction, there must be variation in whether professionals know of the patient's experimental condition. This is best achieved by adding another manipulation to the study. But for practical reasons, there is a very low ceiling to the number of cognate manipulations possible.

Researchers have more chances to add differentiating outcomes measures. In this regard, consider length of hospital stay as a measure of recovery from surgery. Hospital administrators are under pressure from their sources of reimbursement to reduce length of stay and so, for a given diagnosis, hospitals are now only reimbursed for a prespecified number of hospital days. If patients left the hospital sooner because of this financial administrative component of length of stay, they might well be in poorer physical health and so run a greater chance of being rehospitalized or delayed in their return to normal activities at home or work. To distinguish between a genuinely speedier recovery and a premature discharge due to reimbursement policies, valid measures are required of patients' physical conditions on leaving the hospital, their rehospitalization rates, and the time it takes them to resume normal activities. Differentiation between target and cognate outcomes should be widespread in individual studies thanks to the relative ease with which additional outcomes measures can usually be collected.

A component-of-variance approach does not help if the same source of bias runs through all operational instances. Constant bias precludes discovery whether an effect is found when the bias is absent, for it is never absent. It also precludes testing whether the cause-effect relationship is obtained despite heterogeneity in the direction of bias, for there is only homogeneity. Thus, if all the patient education interventions to date had been implemented by researchers rather than regular staff nurses or physicians, this would constitute a serious threat to causal generalization irrespective of the number of past studies and their heterogeneity on other irrelevant attributes. In such a situation, the most the analyst can do is invoke relevant theories, past findings, or any other form of indirect argument that might help assess the likelihood of bias causing the causal connection under analysis. The possibility of constant bias is a major problem in construct validation, precluding both the variance analysis required to empirically rule out alternative interpretations and the less direct forms of falsification based on summation of data across different sources of irrelevancy.

Principle of Causal Explanation. In nomological theories of construct validation (Cronbach and Meehl, 1955), an interpretation of an entity is validated, rather than the entity as such. Thus, anxiety is inferred when a theory successfully predicts the causally efficacious components of multivariate constructs, the factors that cause anxiety measures to vary, the pattern of effects to which anxiety leads, and the processes through which anxiety influences this pattern of effects. Likewise, a theory of socioeconomic status (SES) might specify that its major conceptual components are education, occupation, and income; that occupation is three times more important than the other components; that SES is related to the likelihood of voting for mainstream Republican candidates but not for conservative Evangelicals; and that status is "transmitted" intergenerationally because high-SES parents place greater emphasis on setting goals for their children's educational behavior and on monitoring performance toward these goals. Theoretical predictions like these increase the number of implications associated with a particular interpretation of a construct. As the pattern of expected relationships becomes more complex, the number of alternative explanations decreases. In this conception of construct validation, many more predictions are involved than achieving similarity between a construct description and the sample of items representing that description.

Decomposition of the cause or the effect measures can help with construct validation if the underlying theory specifies which components most increase the prediction of a causal connection. It is rare to find components of a global intervention examined in separate treatment conditions. Within individual studies, our understanding of components is usually achieved through measurement rather than manipulation. As Fisher (1935) pointed out, the perverse implication of this is that treatments should not be rigorously standardized, for only then can naturally occurring variability be used to probe whether a causal conclusion depends on the very components that a substantive theory predicts to be important. Such probes are rarely definitive, however. Respondent characteristics are usually confounded with treatment components, and the procedures currently available for modeling selection are fallible. Even so, careful analysis can help pinpoint which components of a global cause seem most important in bringing about a causal connection and which components of a global effect have been influenced by a treatment.

Explanation plays a crucial role in nomological net theories because researchers are required to specify the ways in which a target construct should be related to other constructs if one interpretation of data outcomes is to be differentiated from others. This is the major function of specifying the antecedents, consequences, and processes associated with a given construct. When theory is precise enough to make such predictions, it is indeed easier to draw inferences about a construct. If we could hypothesize that patient education speeds recovery from surgery with cancer patients but not with others, and that patient education promotes recovery because it increases patients' feelings of self-efficacy, then we could collect the relevant measures, test these hypotheses, and get closer to solving both framings of the causal generalization issue.

But the key question is, To what extent are Cronbach's two types of generalization promoted by the pale approximation to full explanation that social scientists typically achieve? In actual research practice, theoretical concepts and their interrelationships are typically not well sketched, and R^2 values are rarely close to one. It is not easy to use underspecified substantive theory to validate constructs through the specification of antecedents, moderator variables, and mediating processes. However, I want to see more attempts made to do just this, and I believe that some advantages follow from even the marginal gains in explanation that single studies typically achieve.

Principle of Empirical Interpolation and Extrapolation. Nearly all research questions are framed in terms of general cause-and-effect constructs and reference is not made to specific levels of either. Yet, generalization to the constructs themselves requires the assumption that the same causal result holds across all levels of the causal construct and across the full range of the effect. But field experiments with many deliberately manipulated levels of the independent variable are rare. Typically, a few levels are sampled, often only two. The contrast between these, then, has to represent the causal agent writ large. For example, researchers might specify a research question in terms of patient education as the causal factor but then manipulate only an average of three hours of education. Since the control groups will also experience some patient education, the achieved contrast in patient education will be less than three hours—say, two. How likely is it that written research conclusions will refer to the cause either as "three hours of patient education" or as the more exact "two-hour-differential in patient education"? The unqualified construct "patient education" will almost always be invoked as the causal agent.

The ideal solution to this problem emphasizes description of the function relating the full range of patient education to recovery from surgery. This solution entails a dose-response study with independent samples randomly assigned to many patient education levels. This design in turn requires a unidimensional independent variable that can be expressed quantitatively and for which it is practical to vary many levels. These stringent requirements are rarely met in nonlaboratory experimental studies. Multidimensional interventions and few comparison levels are the research reality. The practitioners' dilemma is then to decide how many levels should be chosen.

The minimal situation is to choose two: one level as high or as powerful as is practical and the other equivalent to a no-treatment control group. But then conclusions can only be drawn about the effect of A as it varies between these two levels, not about A more generally. With more resources, a third treatment group could be added that receives more of the treatment than do the controls but less than a high-intensity experimental group. If an effect were then to be observed at both treatment levels, one might conclude that the effect would also have been observed at (unsampled) levels in-between, suggesting an empirically bounded generalization based on interpolation between the two treatment levels and assuming that the cause and the effect are not curvilinearly related within the range studied. If, on the other hand, the data analysis revealed that an effect is found at the higher but not the lower level of the independent variable, this would suggest that the treatment is effective at the higher level but that the causal threshold is higher than the lower level sampled.

Many applied researchers are particularly interested in the level of treatment implementation that would be anticipated as modal if an intervention were to become routinized as formal policy. This emphasis requires selection (and justification) of a treatment level corresponding to the anticipated mode. But this choice alone would not inform us about the treatment when it is implemented at its best, the kind of information that is always a concern of theorists and program developers. Hence, the presumed modal implementation is best incorporated into experimental designs as an intermediate level between high-intensity and no-treatment control conditions. Although this moves the analysis toward description of the functional relationship between the independent and dependent variables (and hence facilitates interpolation), the treatments are often so multidimensional that they cannot be so neatly scaled. Judgment is usually as important as measurement.

A reality of field experimentation is that treatments are seldom implemented in the standardized form associated with best field practice, let alone best laboratory practice. There is nearly always more variability in treatment implementation than originally anticipated. If this variability is measured, analyses can then probe how outcomes are related to the many unplanned levels achieved on the independent variable, though a selection problem arises here because the individuals or sites implementing the treatment at one level may be systematically different from those implementing it at other levels. Nonetheless, this natural variability in treatment implementation can permit testing of whether an effect holds despite the unplanned variability and also of how different treatment levels might be related to the outcome. Without such an analysis, we would know nothing about causal thresholds and other inflection points in the function relating the cause to the effect. Nor would we be able to assess the range within which it seems reasonable to interpolate a causal connection.

Extrapolation is called for when we want to generalize a causal connection beyond the treatment range actually sampled. We might, for example, ask, What effects would patient education have if it were more comprehensive than it has ever been in the past, or if it were provided for one hour per day rather than the thirty minutes per day of past studies? Similar reasoning and assumptions are involved with extrapolation as with interpolation: The more levels there are on the independent variable, and the more systematic the results turn out to be across these levels, the more grounded is the belief that the causal function can be extrapolated beyond either end of the sampled distribution.

However, our confidence in extrapolation decreases as the gap increases between the end of the sampled distribution and the level of desired application. Short extrapolations seem easier to justify, presumably because qualitative transmutations are less likely then—transmutations such as water boiling on reaching one temperature or freezing on reaching another, or a metal cracking when it reaches one temperature or melting when it reaches another, or social relations going from shouting to blows when personal stress escalates. Shorter extrapolations also entail a lower likelihood of exogenous variables coming into play, as when only a very high body temperature brings in the doctor or when only a bank's extreme financial woes bring in special federal auditors. But unless the relevant substantive theory is good enough to specify these points of transmutation—and in my opinion they are rarely so good in the social sciences—there will inevitably be uncertainty about extrapolation, especially when an impressionistically large gap exists between the sampled treatment values and those to which generalization is sought.

Summary. The argument advanced above is that in validating cause and effect constructs, a theory of generalization is involved that is subtly different from both the probability theory buttressing random sampling and the theoretical reductionism underlying most theories of explanation. This alternative uses the description of a target class to guide the selection of instances so that they all belong in the target class and *demonstrably* share most of its prototypical components. Variants among the instances are then purposively selected to rule out the interpretation that the relationship between A and B is due to irrelevancies associated with (1) the methods by which measurement was made, (2) the components that a target construct shares with cognate constructs, (3) the particular levels at which a treatment was manipulated, or (4) any competing substantive interpretations that might be invoked.

The supposition undergirding this approach is that irrelevant interpretations are best ruled out using some form of Mill's Method of Difference. This implies the measurement or manipulation of contending interpretations and an analysis that probes whether an effect remains robust when plausible irrelevancies of a substantive and methodological nature are and are not present. Since it is not easy to specify the full range of competing explanations, inferences about constructs are all the more solid if multiple complex implications of the construct can be specified and tested. The presumption here is that the greater the number of implications corroborated, the less likely are alternative interpretations.

The modified falsificationist approach described above does not require the random sampling of measures or manipulations. Instead, it emphasizes rational selection and the use of data collection and analysis to probe whether a causal relationship remains robust across all of the potential causal contingency variables examined. Random selection of items and manipulations usually can take place within theory-derived strata that correspond with the components presumed to make up a construct. But it is more important to ensure that all theoretically relevant components have been included in the operations and that all irrelevant interpretations can be ruled out. Thus, this elaborate sketch of an alternative to random selection is not an argument against random selection; it is merely an argument about assigning random selection a proper (subsidiary) role in construct validation even when it is feasible. But it is not often feasible.

The Five Principles Applied to Persons and Settings

We now turn to a key question: Are the principles that facilitate generalization to target cause-and-effect constructs also relevant for generalization to target populations of settings and people? These are the domains for which random sampling was originally developed and to which the methods of construct validation have rarely, if ever, been consistently applied. Since random sampling is so rarely feasible when causal connections are involved, we need to know whether these alternative methods of generalization are feasible with people and settings.

Application of the Principle of Proximal Similarity. The principle of proximal similarity is easily dealt with at the individual study level. The instances of people or settings selected for study should fit into the target categories to which generalization is sought, demonstrably incorporating most of the presumed prototypical elements of the category in question. Thus, if the goal is to generalize to patients and physicians within a particular hospital and random selection is not possible, patients or physicians should be chosen from that hospital and should preferably score at or near the hospital mode on measures of demographics, diagnoses (in the case of patients), and training and specialty (in the case of physicians). This is in distinction to selecting persons who belong in the target hospital but use it so seldomly or so idiosyncratically that they are relative outliers (St. Pierre and Cook, 1984).

If the goal were broader and included generalization to all hospitals in the United States, then an alternative might be to select the largest number of hospitals that the budget allows whose size, patient mix, ownership pattern, and the like most closely resemble the national mode. (In cases of multimodality, as with for-profit and not-for-profit hospitals, each mode would need representation.) Modes are best described from archived census sources, where available, or from formally representative samples of a not-too-distant date. If neither is available, more impressionistic sources, such as clinical wisdom, must be critically appraised and used. The purpose of using accidental sampling to represent the mode is to enable researchers to probe a causal relationship among instances that share some of the most salient attributes of the target population. This assigns to representativeness the meaning usually found in theories of categorization rather than of mathematical sampling.

An important issue is how attributes are selected to represent the target category, given that the sampling option under discussion matches on a restricted number of attributes and that, unlike random sampling, there can be no guarantee of matching on unmeasured attributes. In actual research practice, sampling for proximal similarity entails matching the sample and population on easily available measures that are generally considered important in determining performance. Hospital size and ownership pattern probably fit this bill, as do patient age, diagnosis, and method of hospital payment. As Lavori, Louis, Bailar, and Polansky (1986) indicated, samples that have not been selected at random should be described in as much detail as possible. Readers can then assess for themselves, impressionistically, how well the measured attributes of a sample overlap with the known attributes of populations that interest them. This detailed description will let readers know which populations the sample does not represent, and it will give them some idea of what the sample could represent. Unfortunately, it will not delineate what the sample does represent, because matching by proximal similarity involves only a restricted set of the more easily available variables characterizing the population. The population and sample might differ on other attributes that, unbeknownst to the researcher, are differently related to the size or direction of a causal connection. Nonetheless, careful matching can at least ensure that the samples resemble the population on a circumscribed set of characteristics that seems to uniquely describe the populations about which inference is sought.

Application of the Principle of Heterogeneity of Irrelevancies. In sampling modal instances, priority is placed on selecting cases with attributes considered prototypical of a universe. These cases will, of course, differ from each other in a host of different ways, most of them irrelevant to the major research questions. In large sample research, one can probe how robust a causal relationship is across, say, regions of the country, age of the hospital, average tenure of physicians, type of patient diagnosis, or any other patient attributes. If such stratification is not feasible, researchers can at least document the degree of heterogeneity present and can probe whether a cause-effect relationship holds despite this heterogeneity.

Special problems occur, though, when the sample of cases is small, as it is for the setting factor in particular. After all, how many states, hospitals, schools, and the like can a research budget accommodate? Given small samples, an important practical question arises about how to select cases, since heterogeneity can only be deliberately achieved on a small number of irrelevant attributes. Indeed, there are cases where no deliberate sampling for heterogeneity is possible, especially when the guiding research question specifies substantively important moderator variables that have to be included in the sampling design or else the study's major purpose is undermined. For example, imagine that a researcher samples twenty hospitals—ten in each of two treatment groups. After the researcher stratifies on any potential moderator of compelling theoretical or practical interest, little latitude remains for stratifying the hospitals any more finely to deal with a suspected irrelevancy. The researcher can only deal with whatever heterogeneity has been spontaneously generated.

Sampling theorists may throw up their hands at this point and contend that the small samples and plethora of potential causal determinants make sampling theory irrelevant in the hypothetical case mentioned above. I understand and share their exasperation. But limitations like those above regularly confront researchers testing causal propositions with modest budgets. We cannot simply give up on their need for generalized causal influences solely because methodologies based on large samples are not applicable. In the small sample context, there is no perfect algorithm for selecting which variables to make heterogeneous, and I can only advise that it is useful to vary any factor that theoretical speculation or practical wisdom suggests is particularly likely to modify the sign of the relationship between treatment and outcome.

In this regard, it is interesting to note the suggestion of Lavori, Louis, Bailar, and Polansky (1986) that researchers should analyze why individuals and organizations have agreed to participate in a study. Were all the units volunteers? Were they selected because they seemed to be exemplary cases of good practice? Or were the units experiencing special problems and so needed special help? Lavori, Louis, Bailar, and Polansky seem to assign a special status to this set of irrelevant ways in which samples differ from their intended target populations, highlighting them as part of the necessary sample description that substitutes for random selection when the latter is not possible. They are honest here in their struggle to develop a pragmatic, nonstatistical theory of representativeness for many cases where the mathematical sampling theory that they (and I) prefer is not applicable. Their alternative theory of generalization can be expressed in falsificationist terms. The basic hypothesis is that a population of persons or settings is of type X, and this hypothesis is disconfirmed if the sample does not have the prototypical components of population X, or if it has characteristics of Y that are not shared with X, or if the reasons for participating in a study have nothing to do with population X.

As suggested earlier, factors that are research irrelevancies to some persons (for example, universal theorists) may be quite relevant as targets of generalization for others (for example, universe-bound theorists or applied researchers). When resources permit extensive sampling of, say, patients or hospitals, it may be possible to generalize not only to the types of patients or hospitals specified in the guiding research question but also to some of the subtypes of patients or hospitals within the target population—subtypes that may be of special relevance to some research consumers. However, in examining subtypes, researchers must differentiate the types from irrelevancies associated with the particular instances of them that happen to be in a sampling frame. A precondition for this is many instances of the subtype, whether selected randomly or purposively. A trade-off is involved here since, with constant resources, generalization to a broad array of subtypes entails few instances of each subtype, whereas generalization to a smaller number of subtypes entails more units per subtype and hence more stable estimation. Researchers have to decide in advance whether they want to draw strong conclusions about a smaller number of subtypes or weaker conclusions about a larger number of them.

Many basic researchers are disposed to resolve the trade-off between the number of subtypes and the stability of estimation of any one of them in favor of the former. Their assumption is that this choice better approximates universality because a wide range of settings and persons is included in the research base. But other theorists take a different tack. They are prepared to take the results from a single population and assume that broader generalization is warranted until later evidence suggests otherwise (for example, Calder, Phillips, and Tybout, 1981, 1982). Thus, they solve the problem of causal generalization by postponing it for others. This may not be much of a solution for social scientists, however. They lack the tradition of routine, rapid, independent replication that characterizes the world of natural science, and, anyway, some metatheorists of the social sciences assume a particularly complex real world (Cronbach and Snow, 1976; McGuire, 1984). We should be apprehensive about assuming that findings obtained in a single class of settings (for example, the laboratory) with a particular class of persons (for example, college students) will necessarily generalize any further. And we should be loathe to act on the assumption of broad generalization until supportive evidence from heterogeneous replications is available that either has submitted the causal generalization hypothesis to deliberate falsification tests or has at least probed the robustness of a causal relationship across many heterogeneous person and setting types. Unless substantive theory is available that clearly points to factors that are especially likely to condition a causal connection, in my view the best sampling strategy is to select types of persons and settings that cover as wide a range as possible.

Application of the Principle of Discriminant Validity. Clinical lore suggests that cholecystectomy patients are "fair, fat, female, and over forty." If this is true, most respondents in patient education studies are likely to have these same characteristics. Without subsequent analyses, it would therefore not be possible to generalize to cholecystectomy patients with different attributes, though some would undoubtedly be included in the predominantly "fair, fat, female, and over-forty" population. How might effects of gallbladder disease be dissociated with effects of the demographic characteristics of the majority of people with this disease? One possibility requires collecting data on skin color, gender, weight, and age and then conducting data analyses that take these sources of variability into account. If the causal link between patient education and recovery from surgery remained robust across these attributes, we might then conclude that patient education is effective with cholecystectomy patients of all the types examined (the target class) and not just with those having the modal attributes of the class. A separate subanalysis is what promotes such specificity of knowledge.

Discrimination between target populations and their cognates is especially important when claims are made that a particular human population (or setting) is special. To draw conclusions about the unique effects of patient education on, say, prostate cancer sufferers, researchers must differentiate effects found with cancer patients in general from those specific to prostate patients. This discrimination requires a sampling frame with many types of cancer patients and a data analysis that probes whether patient education and recovery are differently related for patients with prostate cancer versus patients with other kinds of cancer. Exclusive study of prostate patients might permit generalization to such patients, but it could never provide enlightenment about how uniquely this group responds to patient education. The same logic holds in discriminating between cancer patients as a class and noncancer patients as a class, or in examining different types of settings. Without the appropriate contrasts there can be no demarcation of what is special about a particular class or type.

Application of the Principle of Causal Explanation. In the present context, causal explanation has to do with understanding why a particular population of persons or settings is implicated in a causal relationship. Part of this explanation has to do with the earlier mentioned process of disaggregating subtypes so as to identify the ranges of persons and settings within the population where a causal relationship can and cannot be demonstrated. But part also has to do with identifying the factors that moderate the causal relationship for a particular population. Thus, if patient education is effective when hospital chaplains implement the programs, is it the denominational similarity between the educator and the patient that is coresponsible for bringing about the effect, or is it the spiritual content of the information transmitted, or is it the chaplain's experience in knowing how to relate to people in need? Answers to questions such as these would help tie down the inference that patient education can be successful when implemented by a chaplain because the causal explanatory data identify processes as much more likely to be associated with chaplains than with other professionals. And once the more causally important attributes of chaplains have been identified, it is then possible to ask whether patient education would be successful with other professionals who have these same attributes and whether these same attributes can be added to the repertoire of existing hospital professionals, thereby facilitating the knowledge transfer called for by Cronbach.

The same reasoning applies to understanding the components of settings. Thus, if a causal connection holds in American hospitals in general, it might be productive to learn what it is about hospitals that brings about the effect. If the answer is related to the presence of persons in them who are frightened by pain and want to control it themselves, then this would be a circumstance rarely met in other parts of U.S. society at large. On the other hand, if a crucial feature turns out to be that hospitals are settings where individuals have considerable time by themselves in which to ponder the advice that patient educators give them, this feature could be made available to other (perhaps as yet unstudied) settings, including nonhospital settings.

Application of the Principle of Empirical Interpolation and Extrapolation. Imagine a causal connection that has been replicated across a wide range on some person or setting variable, as when a relationship is found in the youngest and oldest age groups of respondents or in the smallest and largest hospitals. There is then a temptation to interpolate between the achieved range and conclude that the causal connection would have been found at unsampled intermediate points. This conclusion depends on the linearity of the causal relationship between the sampled extremes and on the absence of other restrictions to the sampling frame, particularly constant biases. In this last connection, consider a study done in the single hospital in Greenwood, Mississippi. Patients might be stratified to achieve a wide range in income, race, age, diagnosis, and comorbidity attributes so that considerable interpolation is possible. But all of the respondents would still be from Greenwood and its surrounds, however heterogeneous or formally representative they might be of that population.

Extrapolation to very broad populations (say, all Americans or all U.S. hospitals) depends both on the heterogeneity of the person or hospital types sampled and on the consistency with which a causal connection is replicated across these types. If a causal connection can be demonstrated across hospitals with many different characteristics and across patients with many different diagnoses, then, by simple induction, it is tempting to infer that the same causal connection is likely to be found with other types of persons and settings not yet tested. The epistemological basis for such generalization is weak, of course. A falsificationist defense of the inference can be constructed, though, on the premise that analysis of a causal relationship across different types of persons or settings provides multiple chances to disconfirm the proposition that a causal relationship is general. If the causal generalization hypothesis is not disconfirmed, then it remains provisionally viable; if it is disconfirmed, then the proposition of causal generalization is rejected and some types of persons or settings have been identified on which the causal conclusion depends. As with all falsification, the hypothesis of causal generality has to be put into conflict with the strongest possible counterhypotheses derived from the theories and experiences of a heterogeneous set of commentators, including some who do not share the primary analyst's theoretical predilections. And the falsification tests also have to be technically adequate within the limits set by our unfortunate predicament that substantive theories are inevitably under-specified and empirical observations are inevitably theory-laden (Cook and Campbell, 1986).

Summary. Useful knowledge about the generalizability of causal conclusions that specify human populations and universes of settings can be drawn without random selection if the same five principles are used that undergird inferences about general cause-and-effect constructs. Random selection is better than the alternative described here, but it is rarely practical in causal research since financial costs, ethics, and the desirability of quality treatment implementation incline researchers toward studies with fewer sites and with the populations of respondents who happen to be in them and have given their consent to be in a study.

Meta-Analysis and the Promotion of Causal Generalization

Most of the prior discussion has been about sampling measurement and data analysis *in single studies*. But few such studies have the large and heterogeneous samples of persons, settings, manipulations, and outcomes measures that our discussion suggests are crucial for the confident assessment of causal generalization. For these we must look to careful, systematic literature reviews. Here, I seek to illustrate the advantages of literature reviews for assessing causal generalization, defending two propositions: (1) One form of review—meta-analysis—is especially well suited to testing general causal propositions. (2) Meta-analysis is so well suited because it uses the five principles elucidated above.

Meta-analysis was originally developed to provide quantitative reviews of studies of the same descriptive causal connections whose generalization we are discussing. It has since been extended to cover such noncausal descriptive questions as "Do boys and girls differ in science achievement or in persuasibility?" And it is now routinely used for identifying factors that moderate a causal connection (Cook, 1991; Cook and others, 1992).

The development of meta-analysis was a response to three major concerns. First, most individual studies of causal phenomena are statistically underpowered (Hedges and Olkin, 1985). Effects have turned out to be more modest than primary researchers anticipated, and so sample sizes have tended to be smaller than needed for reliable detection of effects. Second, to be implementable in practice, individual studies have to build in sampling specifics that limit the range of, say, respondents and treatment implementers, the duration of treatments, the validity of outcomes or moderator measures, and many other specifics that vary from study to study. Third, traditional literature review methods have many flaws, especially the commonly used box-count method of review. This method requires the researcher to tabulate all of the studies that do and do not support a particular causal inference and then to conclude that a causal relationship is general if it is corroborated more often than not. But since statistical significance criteria are usually used to decide whether a causal conclusion is warranted in a particular study, statistically underpowered studies are classified as failing to reject the null hypothesis when, with more respondents and the same effect size, the conclusion would have been exactly the opposite.

These problems were used to justify meta-analysis as a quantitative approach to reviewing the literature. The conduct of a meta-analysis requires at least one effect size from each study, usually a standardized difference between, say, a treatment and a control group on some relevant outcome. Standardization puts study-specific outcomes measures onto the same scale, allowing effect sizes to be averaged across all of the studies sampled. All other things being equal, statistical tests of this average effect size have considerable power because the units are group means and these are more reliable than scores from individual respondents. This may explain why meta-analyses regularly result in average effect sizes that reliably differ from zero, creating in some research areas a much more positive impression about effectiveness than box-count reviews of the same studies have provided.

In good meta-analyses, effect sizes are not just averaged. They are also statistically manipulated like any other observations. Tests can be conducted to see if the distribution of effect sizes is normal; individual studies are weighted to reflect differences in their sample sizes; multivariate tests can be conducted to hold constant any study-level irrelevancies that have been measured; and stratification can take place to assess how a potential modifier has influenced the size or direction of a descriptive causal relationship. Meta-analysis substitutes study-based group-level observations for individual-level observations. Otherwise, little about it is statistically unique.

The effect sizes with which meta-analysts deal are the product of myriad judgments by both primary analysts and meta-analysts. These include judgments about whether to do a study at all, how to design it, whether to write it up, what to include in the write-up, whether to archive the results, and whether to include the study in a review given its topic and methodological quality. Whether fixed- or random-effects models are used, meta-analyses assume that the effect sizes under analysis are drawn at random from the population of all possible effect sizes for a given research question. This assumption is likely to be false and, anyway, cannot be sensitively tested. So meta-analysts emphasize finding "all" of the studies ever conducted on an issue. Yet, even if all of the fugitive studies buried deep in files could be found, this would still constitute a census of all conducted studies and would not represent the more relevant population of all possible studies.

Moreover, reviews are of little use if every published and unpublished study is found but all share the same constant bias. This may have happened, for example, in meta-analyses of how school desegregation affects the academic achievement of black children. Although children stay in school for ten years or more, the available studies cover only the first two years after desegregation (Cook, 1985), probably leading to underestimates of desegregation's total impact. The reality is that meta-analysts work with purposive but heterogeneous samples of studies, the population referents of which are rarely clear and not necessarily devoid of constant biases. Yet, the samples of studies are extremely useful for causal generalization. Why?

Meta-Analytical Use of the Principle of Proximal Similarity. Meta-analysts regularly use the principle of proximal similarity, albeit without the same name. In the absence of a massive (and, from the historian's perspective, probably ephemeral) social consensus that a construct should be measured in a particular way, different researchers tend to measure the same construct in different ways. These differences are not much of a problem if the understanding of the construct is widely shared within a language community, for prototypical components will then be represented in most of the available operational instances and less central components will be less frequently represented. This procedure assigns more weight in the review to prototypical components, enhancing construct validity.

Consider, for example, the approximately 150 studies of patient education reported in the literature (Devine, 1992). The intervention is sometimes provided prior to surgery, sometimes after it, and sometimes at both periods. In some instances, the intervention involves components from only one of the principal domains discussed by theorists: provision of information, skills training, or social support. In other studies, elements from two or three of the domains are combined. But many more studies involve presurgical than involve postsurgical interventions, and many more studies combine intervention components than treat them singly. These are the very emphases represented in most theoretical explications (descriptions and understandings) of the generic patient education construct.

There is no exact pattern match, though. There is no Platonic construct description against which the composite of many single operations can be compared to see if the distribution of weights attached to each component in the theory is matched by the frequency with which components occur across the sample of treatment instances in the literature. At issue is fidelity in gross correspondences between the construct and the relative frequency with which its more or less prototypical components are captured in the literature review. My hypothesis is that this correspondence is better in reviews that contain many operational representations than when relatively few representations are available, as in a single study.

Similar reasoning holds for generalizations about target populations of persons or settings. Proximal similarity is achieved because inclusion in the literature review depends on membership in the target class, say, cholecystectomy patients. Within limits set by errors in recording or diagnosis, all of the respondents in each study are likely to belong in this class. Moreover, the personal attributes most highly correlated with being a cholecystectomy patient (in other words, being fair, fat, female, and over forty) should be distributed more densely across the sample of studies when compared to less prototypical attributes. But how can we know this? In the cholecystectomy example, knowledge of the population attributes comes from clinical lore, though a census or random sample of hospital records would be better. But whatever the source of knowledge about the population, evidence is needed about the extent to which the pattern of patient characteristics in the meta-analysis deviates from the expected profile. A discrepancy suggests the possibility of bias in the studies entering the review, while no discrepancy reduces concern about a lack of representativeness. To show that the samples achieved in a literature review fit into the target category and densely represent its known prototypical attributes, explicit comparisons between population and sample attributes are helpful. For example, Furstenberg, Brooks-Gunn, and Morgan (1987) did these comparisons to support the claim that their sample of Baltimore teenage mothers resembled the national profile of teenage mothers.

Literature reviews do not guarantee generalization to target cause, effect, person, and setting universes. When all of the researchers on a topic share the same understanding of a cause or an effect construct, a bias may result, and future generations may come to see all of their understandings as flawed. Recent claims about the widely shared sexist, racist, ageist, or first-worldist biases of past social scientists illustrate this possibility. On a more mundane level, but illustrating the same basic point, if all of the research on patient education has been performed in Veterans Administration (VA) hospitals, this would constitute a constant bias, however the VA hospitals had been sampled. Reviews are superior to individual studies in their potential to better represent prototypical attributes; but this potential is not a necessary achievement and researchers must continually search to identify hidden sources of constant bias.

Meta-Analytical Use of the Principle of Heterogeneity of Irrelevancies. As far as settings are concerned, a review of cause-probing studies would rarely, if ever, be based on a random sample of hospitals representing, say, the entire United States. Reviewers would have to make do with whatever sample of hospitals turned up in an exhaustive search of published and unpublished sources. Any one hospital—even all of the hospitals in a particular state or region—constitute an irrelevancy for most potential consumers of research findings, and so it is desirable if the hospitals in the review come from all regions of the country and represent many different patterns of ownership, financial health, size, and so on. Since heterogeneity is much greater in the typical review, the potential exists for promoting more confident causal generalizations.

When the number and range of setting variables is impressionistically large, an average effect size can be computed across all of the available types of hospitals to evaluate whether a causal connection is so robust that it persists despite this variability. The analysis also increases the likelihood that a causal connection is not completely confounded with a particular type of hospital, suggesting that the cause-effect link can be found despite the large (but still radically underidentified) variability in the set of hospitals in the review. If researchers are further prepared to assume, perhaps on the basis of reliable background information, that the sampled hospitals are from the most frequently occurring types, then they are even closer to concluding that the effect would also have been found had there been a formally representative sample of hospitals.

But rather than lump together a heterogeneous set of hospitals, it is preferable to create an explicit typology of hospitals and to build these types directly into the data analysis, sample sizes permitting. Probes can then be conducted of whether a causal relationship is found with each type of hospital, region, patient, way of conceptualizing the cause, or whatever (see Devine, 1992). If a causal connection is suggested within one particular type of hospital, say, but not within another, then a contingency variable has been identified that deserves future consideration. This type is not now a causal irrelevancy; rather it is a moderator construct worth further theoretical exploration.

The perfect state of affairs for such analyses is when the sample of units in each stratum or type is large and they are selected at random. But this rarely holds, particularly when large units such as schools or hospitals are involved. Budgets rarely permit experimental interventions into a large number of organizational units. Nonetheless, when they are conducted with sensitivity to the possibility of low statistical power, analyses of a purposively selected and carefully scrutinized sample of instances of a particular type of settings or persons can be used to probe whether a causal connection holds across all of the types examined. Indeed, Devine (1992) did just this, demonstrating a consistent failure to disconfirm the hypothesis of a causal connection from patient education to recovery from surgery across types of patient, types of hospital, time periods, and ways of conceptualizing patient education and recovery from surgery. Such repeated failures in a sample of over 150 studies strengthen the provisional conclusion that patient education has highly generalized causal impacts.

When considering temporal contingencies, the number of studies is often of limited relevance, since the short history of the social sciences limits the time span of studies to the last half century. Even so, the range is far greater in reviews than in individual studies. Devine (1992) was able to show that the size of the causal connection from patient education to recovery from surgery was broadly stable from about 1964 to 1978 but decreased thereafter without shrinking to zero. Computation of an average effect size across the entire period hides this discontinuity in effect sizes (but not causal signs!) and obscures the later years that are particularly important for current deliberation about future health care policy. (Fortunately, Devine was also able to show that the smaller effects in more recent years were probably due to the fact that later studies included fewer components of the global intervention, presumably because researchers felt little need to demonstrate once again the success of global patient education but instead wanted to identify its most efficacious components.)

The enhanced number and range of irrelevancies in reviews also helps promote inferences about target cause-and-effect constructs. The same-labeled cause is manipulated many more ways in a review, while the same-labeled effect is measured in many different ways that reflect researcher-specific understandings and the irrelevancies associated with these. Also evident in the typical review are multiple modes of measurement, different time lags between the manipulation and the outcomes measurement, different kinds of data collectors, and so on. Any causal finding achieved despite such heterogeneity of irrelevancies is all the more firmly anchored conceptually, especially if the individual irrelevancies have been used as stratification variables and the causal connection fails to disappear regardless of whether the heterogeneity is or is not present.

Yet, even this level of confidence can be illusory unless accompanied by vigorous attempts to identify sources of constant bias. For instance, Devine and Cook (1986) showed that nearly all of the patient education studies used researchers rather than regular staff nurses to provide the education treatment. Yet, staff nurses may not be as intensively trained in the intervention as researchers, and they have many more competing responsibilities to contend with in the hospital. Can they ever implement the treatment sufficiently for it to be useful? Regular staff nurses had been used in 4 of the 102 studies reviewed at the time, and effect sizes were smaller in these studies than in those where researchers provided the intervention.

Fortunately, independent evidence showed that the interventions in these 4 studies were less comprehensive than optimal patient education protocols, and a later study conducted with regular nurses and a presumptively powerful treatment achieved the same effect as found in the review (Devine and others, 1988). Even so, the fact that the type of person providing patient education was systematically correlated with treatment intensity across 102 studies suggests that the number of studies in a review is less important than their relevance to conceptual issues. Director (1979) has made the same point about job training, contending that it had been systematically provided to applicants with the worst education and work histories, resulting in a constant source of bias that could not have been controlled for however many similar studies had been conducted.

Some types of meta-analysis welcome more heterogeneity of irrelevancies than do others. Chalmers and his colleagues routinely conduct meta-analyses of available randomized clinical trials of particular drugs or surgical procedures (for example, Chalmers and others, 1988). Their meta-analyses are fairly standardized with respect to independent variables, outcomes measures, experimental designs, diagnoses, physician specialties, and criteria of methodological adequacy for entering the review. Given this strategy, small numbers of studies are likely to result. They can be tolerated, however, since the researchers' major interest is in main effects of the drug or surgical procedure. This research model is close to an exact replication ideal, with the intent being to achieve the clearest possible picture of the causal efficacy of the treatment under conditions designed to maximize the detection of an effect if there is one. Little need seems to be felt to explore the factors that moderate the effects of a drug or surgical procedure.

Contrast this priority with meta-analyses on more social topics in medicine, where the desire is often to assess effectiveness under conditions of real-world implementation, as with such issues as patient education, compliance with drug prescriptions, and effects of psychotherapy. A different attitude toward sources of heterogeneity is then warranted. In patient education, the diagnoses studied meta-analytically are more variable (from transurethral resections of the prostate to limb amputations), the outcomes measures legitimately vary from study to study (length of hospital stay, the amount of pain medication taken, satisfaction with the hospital stay, and so on), and the interventions vary from study to study depending on local understandings of patient education and the time and resources available for more comprehensive versions. In meta-analyses of psychotherapy, the types of therapies and outcomes are even more numerous, as are the patient and therapist types and the institutions in which therapy takes place. Where heterogeneity is the rule, meta-analysts aspire either to generalize across the irrelevancies or to use multivariate procedures to examine how particular sources of heterogeneity influence average effect sizes (see Lipsey, 1992; Shadish, 1992). There is no pretense here of exact replication, or of "pure" tests. Heterogeneity is welcomed to the extent that it maps the heterogeneity in complex social settings of application. Moreover, the greater the heterogeneity in persons, settings, measures, and times examined, the greater the confidence that the cause-effect relationship will also be obtained in still unexamined contexts. Reviews of a sample of standardized studies cannot have this result.

Meta-Analytical Use of the Principle of Discriminant Validity. In their meta-analysis, Devine and Cook (1986) found a subset of studies that permitted discrimination of the target outcome—recovery from surgery—from some of its cognates. This discrimination was possible because the studies measured the time it took patients after their discharge to get back to work or normal activities in their homes. These measures showed that patient education decreased the period required to resume normal activities, thus reducing the plausibility of the argument that the recovery measures tapped the need of hospitals to reduce costs rather than a genuine recovery from surgery. The data on return to normal life indicated that individuals who had experienced patient education were not released prematurely. The larger the sample size of studies, the greater the likelihood of finding some that help unconfound interpretations of the dependent variable. And even if a single study was explicitly designed to achieve such unconfounding, it would inevitably have many other invariant features that would be more likely to vary in a literature review.

The same stratification process also helps interpret the independent variable. For example, a small number of patient education studies included discharge physicians who were blind to the experimental status of respondents. Analysis showed that this blinding made no difference to the size of the link between patient education and recovery from surgery, indicating that physicians' expectations about length of stay did not constitute the causal construct and that patient education might have. The conduct of the analysis required variability in physician expectations, and, all things being equal, we are more likely to find such measures in a review than in any one primary study.

Although multiple studies provide many of the sources of variance needed to discriminate cognate constructs from each other, the number of studies with a particular attribute of interest may be small, as happened with studies of regular staff nurses delivering the patient education treatment. Such small samples make it difficult to estimate whether the available studies differ from the rest of the literature in systematic but irrelevant ways that might be related to the size or sign of a causal connection. When studies with and without an important conceptual attribute are contrasted, this should always be preceded by analyses of the study-level correlates of the attribute's availability. Otherwise, a selection problem can result because the studies with the attribute might be systematically different from other studies in ways that impact effect sizes. This is why multiple-regression analyses are often desirable in which the effects of study-level methodological and theoretical irrelevancies are statistically removed from each study's effect sizes prior to the examination of how a causal relationship might be conditioned by more substantively relevant factors such as hospital size or the nature of the persons implementing a treatment (see Lipsey, 1992).

Meta-Analytical Use of the Principle of Causal Explanation. Researchers explain causal connections in part by identifying the causally effective components of global interventions and the causally affected components of global effects. Meta-analysis allows the researcher to take advantage of the many planned and unplanned sources of variability to explore explanatory possibilities of this sort. For instance, Devine and Cook (1986) were able to decompose the patient education treatment and to isolate the studies that varied in all possible combinations of its three components (provision of information, skills training, and social support). The effects of these different combinations were then assessed, and analyses showed that each component was minimally effective by itself but that combinations of components increased the size of the effect in seemingly additive fashion.

The major limitations to using meta-analysis to identify causally relevant treatment components are practical rather than theoretical. They include the paucity of detail about treatment components in many journals and books (doctoral dissertations prove to be a godsend here!), the published treatment descriptions that are based on what researchers intended to do as an intervention rather than what they actually accomplished, and the need for large samples of studies if sensitive analysis of individual cause-and-effect components is to take place. Nonetheless, there are many published meta-analyses with reasonable probes to identify crucial components of the more global cause-and-effect constructs (for example, Lipsey, 1992).

Full explanation goes way beyond identification of causally efficacious or impacted components. It also requires analysis of the micromediating causal processes that take place after a cause has varied and before an effect has occurred. Although there is nothing in theory to prevent meta-analyses resulting in strong inferences about micromediation, in practice exemplary studies are few and far between (for an exception, see Harris and Rosenthal, 1984; for a broader discussion, see Cook and others, 1992). The reasons for the dearth of positive examples are that (1) one researcher rarely measures the same explanatory processes as another, given how underspecified so many theories are and how strong the social pressures on researchers are to be original; (2) some researchers prefer a black box theory of experimentation and do not want to specify or measure intervening processes; (3) substantive theories are dynamic and change with time, often going through cycles in which old explanatory theories (and their constructs) are disparaged and hence not measured in the next wave of studies; and (4) when data on explanatory variables are collected, they are not always reported in journals in a correlational form that lends itself to synthesis. Such data are usually presented as regression coefficients whose value depends on other variables in the causal model, and models are rarely identical across studies. Hence, meta-analysts cannot use the data to assign *comparable* descriptive relationships to an explanatory construct from one study to the next. These limitations are severe and not likely to go away soon.

Nonetheless, coarse probes of micromediations are possible and promise to provide clues about causal mediation. Many more, and better, clues are possible, though, about person, setting, time, and method factors that moderate a causal relationship. Today's explanatory payoff from meta-analysis should be expected in identifying causal moderator variables rather than causal mediators.

Meta-Analytical Use of the Principle of Empirical Interpolation and Extrapolation. With regard to interpolation and extrapolation, meta-analysis once again holds more promise than any individual study. This is partly because of the wider range typically achieved on many of the person, setting, and time variables worthy of study. Thus, if patient education were effective with medical diagnoses that lead to both very short and very long-term hospital stays, we would be confident in interpolating to types of surgery in between these extremes. This would also be the case if a basic causal finding held with older and younger patients and with the most financially sound and financially imperiled hospitals. And since the extremes are likely to be further apart in a review, the levels represented in any one study are more likely to fall within the extremes achieved across all of the studies. This increases the role that interpolation plays in generalizations about causal connections and decreases the role of the more problematic extrapolation.

Individual studies differ from each other on such internal criteria as the levels of an independent variable, patient characteristics such as SES or age, and organizational features such as hospital size or maturity. These differences can be used to approximate dose-response relationships in order to probe how effect sizes are related, not only to levels of a treatment but also to levels on variables assessing patient and organizational characteristics. The aim is to describe the overall function and any thresholds where the size of the causal relationship suddenly changes, under the assumption that all study-level methodological irrelevancies have been statistically removed from the effect sizes. Since we can never know when this has been successfully accomplished, special interpretive weight needs to be given to the subset of individual studies where multiple levels of the treatment were experimentally varied or where multiple levels of a person or setting contingency variable were deliberately measured. But even when such within-study comparisons cannot be made, it is still desirable to take advantage of the greater variability that reviews offer to probe the functional form of a cause-and-effect relationship across person and setting attributes as well as across treatment levels.

Summary. A literature review technique such as meta-analysis enhances causal generalization because it has built into it five principles that promote such generalization. It deals with proximal similarity better than any single study could because, all other things being equal, it distributes the prototypical elements of the cause, effect, person, and setting constructs more densely throughout the sample of studies. Reviews also contain many more sources of methodological and substantive heterogeneity that permit analysts to assess how robust a causal relationship is when these sources of heterogeneity are combined, and when it is separately examined across a wide range of person, setting, and time factors as well as across many different ways of measuring a cause or effect. Robust findings do more than merely identify the populations to which generalization is warranted. They are also more likely to be reproducible in as yet unstudied circumstances, thereby facilitating Cronbach's second type of causal generalization. However, the empirical cross-population generalization that meta-analysis emphasizes is quite different from the more theory-based cross-population generalization that Cronbach's theory treats as most important.

Reviews also promise better discrimination among cognate constructs, in part because reviews are more likely to include studies with constructs or populations that differ from the mode. Thus, for example, any one study is likely to have cholecystectomy patients who are "fair, fat, female, and over forty," thereby confounding the diagnosis "cholecystectomy patient" with the demographic category "women of North European extraction." But a review is more likely to have one or more studies with unique demographic groups and one or more studies where the data have been reported for cholecystectomy patients with different demographic profiles. But discrimination of the sort that we are considering is not limited to modal attributes. For instance, in a review there is also a greater likelihood of discovering one or more studies with measures of the time that it takes to return to work after surgery, permitting us to differentiate patient recovery from premature hospital releases.

Reviews are also superior for interpolation because a broader range— and many more levels—are achieved on variables of interest. And, finally, reviews offer special benefits for causal explanation because the variability in measures enhances the ability to discover the causally efficacious components of the global cause, the causally impacted components of the effect, and many of the variables that modify a causal connection of interest. It is more difficult to use meta-analysis for identifying causal mediating variables, however. But this is more for practical reasons than because of limits intrinsic to meta-analysis.

Conclusion

Cronbach's First Framing of the Causal Generalization Issue. The first purpose of this chapter was to examine the roles of random selection in facilitating generalized inferences about the connection between a treatment and an outcome. Such inferences require us to make valid statements about treatments, outcomes, persons, settings, times, and the nature of the link between a treatment and an outcome. My analysis led to a somewhat pessimistic conclusion. When probing causal connections in individual studies, random sampling is sometimes practical with persons, but it is rarely, if ever, possible with treatments, settings, outcomes, or times. Even with persons, random selection is usually from within a small and circumscribed collection of settings that have been selected more for their logistical and financial convenience than for their formal representativeness in a sampling theory sense.

Another purpose of this chapter was to describe an alternative theory of causal generalization built around five principles abstracted from research on construct validation, where the task is to generalize from measures and empirical relationships to theoretical constructs, particularly cause-and-effect constructs. Much can already be done within individual studies to promote causal generalization by (1) purposively sampling proximally similar instances; (2) making irrelevancies more heterogeneous and stratifying to see if they make a difference, thereby assessing some of the person, setting, time, and method factors across which a causal connection can and cannot be obtained; (3) stratifying on cognate variables to differentiate them from the target populations of research interest; (4) identifying the ranges within which a causal relationship does and does not hold; and (5) describing the components of the cause and the effect and any other variables that might moderate or mediate a causal connection, thereby helping explain why a cause and an effect are linked.

These five principles do not enjoy as strong a logical warrant as random sampling. To produce interpretable results, they require target categories that are clearly described, prototypical attributes that can be clearly delineated, and alternatives that can be ruled out in regard to preferred interpretations of the populations and constructs. This last requirement is the most difficult to satisfy. However, it is approximated when a causal conclusion is robust across all known irrelevancies, when the influence of target constructs can be differentiated from those of cognate constructs with overlapping attributes, and when target constructs or populations are demonstrably not confounded with particular values on these entities. This is a daunting set of conditions, which are better met in literature reviews than in individual studies. Literature reviews should be the primary source for confident conclusions about causal generalization.

This alternative theory emphasizes purposive sampling for theoretical ends rather than random sampling to represent a population. The sampling is designed to capture various features that promote generalization: prototypical attributes, heterogeneity on theoretically peripheral attributes, discrimination of target from cognate constructs, identification of important components and moderator variables, and extension of the range on many variables where interpolation is called for. Random selection is much less important in this conception, though welcome when it can be achieved. Since random selection is the linchpin of sampling theory, what I have advocated lies outside the bounds of formal sampling theory. Just as Campbell had to explicate what random assignment to treatments controls for in order to develop his theory of quasi experimentation, so I have had to explicate what random selection achieves in order to explore alternative (and messier) ways of bringing about the same ends.

In my analysis, what random selection does is match a sample and population on prototypical attributes, rule out alternative interpretations because irrelevancies are distributed in the sample as in the population, and discriminate between target and cognate populations since only the target enters the sampling frame; and it allows researchers to probe whether various subpopulations relate to research outcomes in the same way, thus promoting causal explanation. But while random selection accomplishes these goals principally via a procedure, the sampling designs advocated here depend on theoretical stratification on variables that helps promote causal generalization and on selection of a purposive sample of cases within each stratum. No pretense can be made, therefore, that causal generalization is "automatic." It is a difficult inference, related more to attempts to disconfirm the hypothesis of causal generalization than to claims of generalization based solely on the sampling procedure used. In this sense, my approach is a quasi-sampling theory of causal generalization.

Overall, I do not want to claim too much for the five principles outlined here. No theory of causal generalization is currently available that is so logically warranted, so empirically probed, so comprehensive in coverage, and so practically superior to the currently available alternatives that it merits hegemony for research practice. Instead, multiple methods for causal generalization will be needed to meet the criteria listed above, and much theoretical work will need to be undertaken to modify and extend these criteria. Given that no simple but practical theory of causal generalization currently exists, critical multiplism (Cook, 1985; Shadish, 1989) should be the motto and methodological dogmatism the fear.

Cronbach's Second Framing of the Causal Generalization Issue. Many scholars and practitioners are interested in Cronbach's second framing of the causal generalization issue: "How to justify generalizations from entities with certain characteristics to entities with quite different characteristics?" This is not the same as the traditional meta-analysis question: "Across which examined population is a particular causal conclusion warranted?" Although both questions involve cross-population generalization, in only one case does the intended inference go beyond characteristics of the available samples to include conclusions about novel causal connections and novel contexts where a causal connection may never have been studied before. Transfer of knowledge to new circumstances lies at the heart of this second framing of the causal generalization issue.

Explanation is usually invoked as the preferred method for learning about causal transfer. The presumption is that once we know why or how a cause-effect relationship comes about, we can then identify the conditions that seem necessary and sufficient for the effect, permitting us to bring these conditions together in novel treatment configurations that are tailored to the specifics of particular local populations and local settings. For those scholars who reject the language of necessary and sufficient conditions (Cook and Campbell, 1979), causal transfer is enhanced whenever we learn about the moderator and mediator variables that condition a causal connection. Such knowledge should help practitioners decide whether the major causal facilitants are present in the settings for which they are responsible.

We need not question the premise that causal explanation promotes the transfer of research findings. Indeed, I have claimed as much here, even adding that causal explanation can promote causal generalization in Cronbach's first framing as well as his second. But I did contend that some uncertainty is warranted about whether, in actual social science practice, causal explanation can reliably play the transfer role ascribed to it. It seems to me that few social science theories are precise enough in the moderator and mediator constructs invoked, and that the gains in explanation we typically achieve in individual studies identify one or two causal contingency variables rather than identify all or most of the necessary and sufficient conditions for an effect. Cronbach is so sensitive to this shortfall between the promise of causal explanation and the causal explanatory gains likely to be achieved using today's methods that he advocates the pursuit of causal explanation through a variety of methods, many of which are more akin to common sense than to the quantitative causal modeling techniques whose results he finds so model-dependent.

Meta-analysis offers a different route to causal generalization in both of Cronbach's senses. Given a heterogeneous array of studies, meta-analysis permits empirical probes of the robustness of a causal connection across subtypes of the cause and the effect and across different types of persons, settings, and times. The greater the heterogeneity in such variables and the greater the consistency of results achieved, the stronger is the presumption that the same relationship will be found with quite different populations of persons, settings, and times and with variants of the cause and the effect that are not identical to those studied to date. Although many scientists assume broad causal generalization after only a few demonstrations, my preference is to undertake heterogeneous replications of the causal proposition under test. If the hypothesis of causal generalization remains robust despite all these falsification attempts, and if no plausible alternative interpretations remain to the generalization hypothesis, then this is a stronger base for inferring that results can be transferred elsewhere.

Meta-analysis is relatively successful in promoting causal generalization because its practitioners operate within an intellectual framework that emphasizes (1) sampling for proximal similarity rather than formal representativeness, (2) description and analysis of heterogeneous sources of theoretical irrelevancy, (3) discrimination of target constructs from their cognates, (4) sampling of substantively meaningful third variables to probe whether they condition a causal connection, and (5) identification of the causally efficacious components of a treatment class, the causally impacted components of an effect category, and any factors that might mediate the relationship between the two (Cook and others, 1992).

References

Bandura, A. *Social Foundations of Thought and Action: A Social Cognitive Theory.* Englewood Cliffs, N.J.: Prentice Hall, 1986.

Bhaskar, R. *A Realist Theory of Science.* Leeds, England: Leeds, 1975.

Brunswik, E. *Perception and the Representative Design of Psychological Experiments.* (2nd ed.) Berkeley: University of California Press, 1955

Calder, B. J., Phillips, L. W., and Tybout, A. M. "Designing Research for Application." *Journal of Consumer Research,* 1981, *8,* 197–207.

Calder, B. J., Phillips, L. W., and Tybout, A. M. "The Concept of External Validity." *Journal of Consumer Research,* 1982, *9,* 240–244.

Campbell, D. T. "Factors Relevant to the Validity of Experiments in Social Settings." *Psychological Bulletin,* 1957, *54,* 297–312.

Campbell, D. T. "Artifact and Control." In R. Rosenthal and R. L. Rosnow (eds.), *Artifact in Behavioral Research.* San Diego: Academic Press, 1969.

Campbell, D. T. "Qualitative Knowing in Action Research." In M. Brenner and P. Marsh (eds.), *The Social Contexts of Method.* London: Croon-Helm, 1978.

Campbell, D. T., and Fiske, D. W. "Convergent and Discriminant Validation by the Multitrait-Multimethod Matrix." *Psychological Bulletin,* 1959, *56,* 81–105.

Campbell, D. T., and Stanley, J. C. *Experimental and Quasi-Experimental Designs for Research.* Skokie, Ill.: Rand McNally, 1966.

Chalmers, T. C., and others. "Meta-Analysis of Randomized Controlled Trials as a Method of Estimating Rare Complications of Non-Steroidal Anti-Inflammatory Drug Therapy." In *Alimentary and Pharmacological Therapy,* 1988.

Collingwood, R. G. *An Essay on Metaphysics.* Oxford, England: Clarendon, 1940.

Cook, T. D. "Postpositivist Critical Multiplism." In L. Shotland and M. M. Mark (eds.), *Social Science and Social Policy.* Newbury Park, Calif.: Sage, 1985.

Cook, T. D. "Meta-Analysis: Its Potential for Causal Description and Causal Explanation with Program Evaluation." In G. Albrecht, H.-U. Otto, S. Karstedt-Henke, and K. Bollert (eds.),

Social Prevention and the Social Sciences: Theoretical Controversies, Research Problems and Evaluation Strategies. New York: Walter de Gruyter, 1991.

Cook, T. D., and Campbell, D. T. (eds.). *Quasi-Experimentation: Design and Analysis Issues for Field Settings.* Boston: Houghton Mifflin, 1979.

Cook, T. D., and Campbell, D. T. "The Causal Assumptions of Quasi-Experimental Practice." *Synthese,* 1986, *68,* 141–180.

Cook, T. D., Leviton, L., and Shadish, W. R., Jr. "Program Evaluation." In G. Lindzey and E. Aronson (eds.), *Handbook of Social Psychology.* (3rd ed.) New York: Knopf, 1985.

Cook, T. D., and others. *Meta-Analysis for Explanation: A Casebook.* New York: Russell Sage Foundation, 1992.

Cronbach, L. J. *Designing Evaluations of Educational and Social Programs.* San Francisco: Jossey-Bass, 1982.

Cronbach, L. J. "Construct Validation After Thirty Years." Paper presented at the symposium "Intelligence: Measurement, Theory, and Public Policy," Urbana, Illinois, May 1985.

Cronbach, L. J., Ambron, S. R., Dombusch, S. M., Hess, R. D., Hornik, R. C., Phillips, D. C., Walker, D. F., and Weiner, S. S. *Toward Reform of Program Evaluation: Aims, Methods, and Institutional Arrangements.* San Francisco: Jossey-Bass, 1980.

Cronbach, L. J., Gleser, G. C., Nanda, H., and Rajaratram, N. *The Dependability of Behavioral Measurements: Theory of Generalizability for Scores and Profiles.* New York: Wiley, 1972.

Cronbach, L. J., and Meehl, P. E. "Construct Validity in Psychological Tests." *Psychological Bulletin,* 1955, *52,* 281–302.

Cronbach, L. J., Rajaratram, N., and Gleser, G. C. *The Dependability of Behavioral Measurements: Multifacet Studies of Generalizability.* Stanford, Calif.: Stanford University Press, 1967.

Cronbach, L. J., and Snow, R. E. *Aptitudes and Instructional Methods.* New York: Irvington, 1976.

Devine, E. C. "Effects of Psychoeducational Care with Adult Surgical Patients: A Theory-Probing Meta-Analysis of Intervention Studies." In T. D. Cook and others (eds.), *Meta-Analysis for Explanation: A Casebook.* New York: Russell Sage Foundation, 1992.

Devine, E. C., and Cook, T. D. "A Meta-Analytic Analysis of Effects of Psychoeducational Interventions on Length of Post-Surgical Hospital Stay." *Nursing Research,* 1983, *32* (5), 267–274. ·

Devine, E. C., and Cook, T. D. "Clinical and Cost Relevant Effects of Psychoeducational Interventions: A Meta-Analysis." *Research in Nursing and Health,* 1986, *9,* 89–105.

Devine, E. C., and others. "Clinical and Financial Effects of Psychoeducational Care Provided by Staff Nurses to Adult Surgical Patients in the Post-DRG Environment." *American Journal of Public Health,* 1988, *78,* 1293–1297.

Director, S. M. "Underadjustment Bias in the Evaluation of Manpower Training." *Evaluation Quarterly,* 1979, *3,* 190–218.

Fisher, R. A. *The Design of Experiments.* London: Oliver and Boyd, 1935.

Furstenberg, F. F., Jr., Brooks-Gunn, J., and Morgan, S. P. *Adolescent Mothers in Later Life.* New York: Cambridge University Press, 1987.

Gasking, D. "Causation and Recipes." *Mind,* 1957, *64,* 479–487.

Glass, G. V., McGaw, B., and Smith, M. L. *Meta-Analysis in Social Research.* Newbury Park, Calif.: Sage, 1981.

Glymour, C. *Discovering Causal Structure: Artificial Intelligence, Philosophy of Science, and Statistical Modelling.* San Diego: Academic Press, 1987.

Harris, M. J., and Rosenthal, R. "Mediation of Interpersonal Expectancy Effects: 31 Meta-Analyses." *Psychological Bulletin,* 1984, *97,* 363–386.

Hedges, L. V., and Olkin, I. *Statistical Methods for Meta-Analysis.* San Diego: Academic Press, 1985.

Kish, L. *Statistical Design for Research.* New York: Wiley, 1987.

Kruglanski, A. W., and Kroy, M. "Outcome Validity in Experimental Research: A Re-Conceptualization." *Journal of Representative Research in Social Psychology*, 1975, 7, 168–178.

Kuhn, T. S. *The Structure of Scientific Revolutions*. Chicago: University of Chicago Press, 1962.

Lakoff, G. *Women, Fire, and Dangerous Things: What Categories Reveal About the Mind*. Chicago: University of Chicago Press, 1987.

Lammlein, S. E., Peterson, N. G., and Rosse, R. L. "Pilot Test of a Probabilistic Sampling Critical Task Selection Model for Performance Testing." Minneapolis, Minn.: Personnel Decisions Research Institute, 1987.

Lavori, P. W., Louis, T. A., Bailar, J. C., and Polansky, H. "Designs for Experiments: Parallel Comparisons of Treatment." In J. C. Bailar and F. Mosteller (eds.), *Medical Uses of Statistics*. Waltham, Mass.: New England Journal of Medicine, 1986.

Lipsey, M. W. "Juvenile Delinquency Treatment: A Meta-Analytic Inquiry into the Variability of Effects." In T. D. Cook and others (eds.), *Meta-Analysis for Explanation: A Casebook*. New York: Russell Sage Foundation, 1992.

McGuire, W. J. "Contextualism." In L. Berkowitz (ed.), *Advances in Experimental Social Psychology*. San Diego: Academic Press, 1984.

Mackie, J. L. *The Cement of the Universe: A Study of Causation*. Oxford, England: Oxford University Press, 1974.

Mark, M. M. "Validity Typologies and the Logic and Practice of Quasi-Experimentation." In W.M.K. Trochim (ed.), *Advances in Quasi-Experimental Design and Analysis*. New Directions for Program Evaluation, no. 31. San Francisco: Jossey-Bass, 1986.

O'Connor, F. W., and others. "Enhancing Implementation of Surgical Nurses' Psycho-educational Care: Effects of a Research-Based Workshop." Unpublished manuscript, School of Nursing, University of Wisconsin, Milwaukee, 1989.

Riecken, H. W., and Boruch, R. F. (eds.). *Social Experimentation*. San Diego: Academic Press, 1974.

Rosch, E. H. "Principles of Categorization." In E. H. Rosch and B. B. Lloyd (eds.), *Cognition and Categorization*. Hillsdale, N.J.: Erlbaum, 1978.

St. Pierre, R. G., and Cook, T. D. "Sampling Strategy in the Design of Program Evaluations." In R. F. Conner, D. G. Altman, and C. Jackson (eds.), *Evaluation Studies Review Annual*. Vol. 9. Newbury Park, Calif.: Sage, 1984.

Shadish, W. R., Jr. "Private-Sector Care for Chronically Mentally Ill Individuals: The More Things Change, the More They Stay the Same." *American Psychologist*, 1989, 44 (8), 1142–1147.

Shadish, W. R., Jr. "Do Family and Marital Psychotherapies Change What People Do? A Meta-Analysis of Behavioral Outcomes." In T. D. Cook and others (eds.), *Meta-Analysis for Explanation: A Casebook*. New York: Russell Sage Foundation, 1992.

Smith, E. E., and Medin, D. E. *Categories and Concepts*. Cambridge, Mass.: Harvard University Press, 1981.

Stegmuller, W. *The Structure and Dynamics of Theories*. New York: Springer-Verlag, 1976.

Warnecke, J. R., and others. "Characteristics of Participants in a Televised Smoking Cessation Intervention." *Journal of Preventive Medicine*, 1991, 20, 389–403.

Warnecke, R. B., and others. "The Second Chicago Televised Smoking Cessation Program: A 24-Month Follow-Up." *American Journal of Public Health*, 1992, 82, 835–840.

Webb, E. J., Campbell, D. T., Schwartz, R. D., and Sechrest, L. B. *Unobtrusive Measures*. Skokie, Ill.: Rand McNally, 1966.

Wigdor, A. K., and Green, B. F., Jr. (eds.). *Assessing the Performance of Enlisted Personnel: Evaluation of a Joint-Service Research Project*. Washington, D.C.: National Academy Press, 1986.

THOMAS D. COOK is professor of sociology, psychology, education, and public policy at the Center for Urban Affairs and Policy Research, Northwestern University, Evanston, Illinois.

INDEX

Rajaratram, N., 46, 80
Random sampling, in causal generalization, 42, 44; and cause-and-effect constructs, 45–47, 58–59, 76–77; *versus* judgmental item sampling, 46; limitations of, 49; and populations, 47–49; and proximal similarity sampling, 50
Randomized experimentation, 1, 25. *See also* Random sampling
Reductionism, 58
Refusal, of treatment, 47–48
Reichardt, C. S., 6, 29, 37
Replication, of research, 71
Research design: black box *versus* theory approach to, 9–10; role of theory in, 15–24. *See also* Methodology; Quasi-experimental research
Research paradigms: differentiated, 8–9; minimalist, 7–8. *See also* Black box paradigm; Treatment theory
Resistance, to treatment, 18
Rezmovic, E. L., 17, 37
Riecken, H. W., 46, 81
Rindskopf, D., 31, 37
Rival explanations, elimination of, 28–31
Rosch, E. H., 49, 81
Rosen, A., 27, 37
Rosenthal, R., 73, 80
Rosse, R. L., 46, 81
Rossi, P. H., 7, 9, 10, 11, 14, 15, 17, 18, 20, 31, 35, 37
Rubin, D. B., 5, 37
Runyan, W. M., 14, 37

St. Pierre, R. G., 30, 37, 59, 81
Sample size, and statistical power, 21. *See also* Sampling theory; Target populations
Sampling theory, and causal generalization, 2, 42–43, 45–49, 61, 65–66, 77. *See also* Random sampling
Scheirer, M. A., 11, 17, 37
Schneider, A. L., 20, 37
Schwartz, R. D., 45, 49, 81
Scott, Anne G., 1–3
Scriven, M., 19, 27, 37
Sechrest, L. B., 1–3, 9, 11, 16, 17, 20, 21, 27, 31, 37, 38, 45, 49, 81
Settings, in causal generalization, 40, 41; and meta-analysis, 68–69; and principles for cause-and-effect constructs, 59–65; random sampling and, 47–49

Sex crimes, study on, 30
Shadish, W. R., Jr., 43, 71, 77, 80, 81
Shapiro, J. Z., 37, 19, 30, 38
Sherrill, S., 19, 38
Side effects. *See* Outcome variables
Side studies, 33
Small group leadership theory, 13
Smith, A., 23, 38
Smith, E. E., 44, 81
Smith, M. L., 44, 80
Snow, R. E., 52, 62, 80
Snowden, L. R., 18, 38
Social learning theory, 13
Social sciences: background theory in, 12; causal explanation in, 44, 46, 78; causal generalization in, 52–53, 62; evaluation in, 1; and meta-analysis, 71–72; treatment effectiveness research in, 7–8. *See also* Psychotherapy
Socioeconomic status, study of, 54–55
Stage-state analysis, 14–15
Stanford Heart Disease Prevention Project, 14
Stanley, J. C., 24, 35, 45, 79
Statistical methodology: for causal generalization, 42–43; for detection of treatment effects, 20–24. *See also* Sampling theory
Stegmuller, W., 51, 81
Stochastic factors, 11–12
Stouthamer-Loeber, M., 17, 36
Stratification, 72. *See also* Subtypes
Strauss, A. L., 13, 36
Subjects: attrition of, 30–31, 47; issues about, 17–18; and motivation, 61; and outcomes measurement, 23–24; volunteers as, 24, 61. *See also* Target populations
Substantive model, 15
Subtypes, identification of, 61–62, 63, 69–70
Suchman, E. A., 31, 38

Taber, M. A., 15, 38
Target cause/effect/setting, 41. *See also* Target populations
Target populations: in causal generalization, 40, 41; definition of, 17–18; and meta-analysis, 68; and principles for cause-and-effect constructs, 59–65; and random sampling, 45, 47–49; and transfer of knowledge, 43–44, 63, 78.

Ordering Information

New Directions for Program Evaluation is a series of paperback books that presents the latest techniques and procedures for conducting useful evaluation studies of all types of programs. Books in the series are published quarterly in Spring, Summer, Fall, and Winter and are available for purchase by subscription as well as by single copy.

Subscriptions for 1993 cost $48.00 for individuals (a savings of 20 percent over single-copy prices) and $70.00 for institutions, agencies, and libraries. Please do not send institutional checks for personal subscriptions. Standing orders are accepted.

Single copies cost $17.95 when payment accompanies order. (California, New Jersey, New York, and Washington, D.C., residents please include appropriate sales tax.) Billed orders will be charged postage and handling.

Discounts for quantity orders are available. Please write to the address below for information.

All orders must include either the name of an individual or an official purchase order number. Please submit your order as follows:
Subscriptions: specify series and year subscription is to begin
Single copies: include individual title code (such as PE1)

Mail all orders to:
Jossey-Bass Publishers
350 Sansome Street
San Francisco, California 94104

For single-copy sales outside of the United States contact:
Maxwell Macmillan International Publishing Group
866 Third Avenue
New York, New York 10022

For subscription sales outside of the United States, contact
any international subscription agency or Jossey-Bass directly.

OTHER TITLES AVAILABLE IN THE
NEW DIRECTIONS FOR PROGRAM EVALUATION SERIES
William R. Shadish, *Editor-in-Chief*